Coaches Guide to
SPORT ADMINISTRATION

A publication for the
American Coaching Effectiveness Program
Master Series Sport Management Curriculum

Larry M. Leith, PhD
University of Toronto

Leisure Press
Champaign, Illinois

Library of Congress Cataloging-in-Publication Data

Leith, Larry M., 1949-
　　Coaches guide to sport administration / Larry M. Leith.
　　　　p.　　cm.
　　"A publication for the American Coaching Effectiveness Program,
　　master series sport management curriculum."
　　Includes bibliographical references.
　　ISBN 0-88011-379-0
　　1. Coaching (Athletics)　2. Sports--Organization and
　　administration.　I. American Coaching Effectiveness Program.
　　II. Title.
　　GV711.L45　1990　　71352
　　796'.07'7--dc20　　　　　　　　　　　　　　　　89-39169
　　　　　　　　　　　　　　　　　　　　　　　　　　　CIP

ISBN: 0-88011-379-0

Developmental Editor: Linda Anne Bump, PhD
Copyeditor: Barbara Walsh
Assistant Editor: Julia Anderson
Proofreader: Bruce Owens
Production Director: Ernie Noa
Typesetter: Sandra Meier
Text Design: Keith Blomberg
Text Layout: Denise Lowry
Interior Art: Timothy Stiles and Gretchen Walters
Printer: Versa Press

Printed in the United States of America

10　9　8　7　6　5　4　3　2　1

Leisure Press
A Division of Human Kinetics Publishers, Inc.
Box 5076, Champaign, IL 61825-5076
1-800-747-4457

ACEP Master Series Courses

ACEP Master Series courses are available to accompany the following texts.

Sport Science

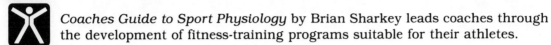

Coaches Guide to Sport Psychology by Rainer Martens discusses motivation, communication, leadership, and how to develop a variety of psychological skills.

Coaches Guide to Sport Physiology by Brian Sharkey leads coaches through the development of fitness-training programs suitable for their athletes.

Coaches Guide to Teaching Sport Skills by Robert Christina and Daniel Corcos uses practical examples to take coaches through the teaching/learning process.

Coaches Guide to Nutrition and Weight Control by Patricia Eisenman, Stephen Johnson, and Joan Benson provides practical guidelines to help coaches assist athletes in losing, gaining, or maintaining weight safely.

Coaches Guide to Social Issues in Sport by Jay Coakley and Robert Hughes examines how age, race, gender, and culture influence sport participation.

Coaches Guide to Sport Biomechanics describes the mechanical principles involved in sport movements.

Sports Medicine

Coaches Guide to Sport Injuries by J. David Bergeron and Holly Wilson Greene gives coaches information on injury prevention, emergency care, and follow-up procedures.

Coaches Guide to Sport Rehabilitation by Steven Tippett explains both the coach's role in rehabilitation and the process of rehabilitation as directed by health-care professionals.

Coaches Guide to Drugs and Sport examines the effects of a variety of abused drugs and the coach's role in combatting drug use.

Sport Management

Coaches Guide to Sport Law by Gary Nygaard and Thomas Boone explains the coach's legal duties in easy-to-understand terms.

Coaches Guide to Time Management by Charles Kozoll explains how to improve organization and avoid time-related stresses.

Coaches Guide to Sport Administration by Larry Leith provides guidelines to help coaches plan, organize, lead, and control their team's success.

Each course consists of a *Coaches Guide, Study Guide*, and *Workbook*. ACEP certification is awarded for successful course completion. For more information, please contact

ACEP
Box 5076
Champaign, IL 61825-5076
1-800-747-4457

Contents

Preface

The primary purpose of the *Coaches Guide to Sport Administration* is to focus on the development of administrative skills that can lead to more efficient coaching. In easy-to-read terms, this *Guide* presents the administrative duties you have as a coach. The content is drawn from a thorough review of administrative principles that have direct bearing on coaching behavior. In each case, the administrative technique is developed by integrating the principle under consideration into specific coaching examples. Although this administrative guide is written specifically for coaches, the nature of the text makes it valuable for physical educators and sport administrators as well.

The general organization of the *Guide* includes eight chapters of instruction. Chapter 1 introduces the concept of coaching administration. Here, you are introduced to the three essential skills of coaching and presented with an overview of the underlying administrative principles that are developed throughout the *Guide*. Chapters 2 through 7 examine the administrative processes of planning, organizing, leading, and controlling. These chapters, which make up a major portion of the text, provide you with specific administrative skills that will effectively focus your coaching behavior. Specifically, chapters 4 and 5 are helpful guides to organizing fund-raisers and competitions, areas that concern many coaches. Chapter 8 deals with techniques of decision making. In this section, you will be exposed to procedures that can minimize the number of day-to-day decisions that you must make. Finally, a conclusion section summarizes the major premises of the *Guide* and forecasts factors that will place greater demands on your administrative skills in the future.

Rather than approaching administration from the standpoint of a long list of dos and don'ts, this *Guide* encourages you to focus on specific administrative functions that can lead to improved coaching ability.

"Would you tell me, please, which way I ought to go from here?"

"That depends a good deal on where you want to get to," said the Cat.

"I don't care much where . . ." said Alice.

"Then it doesn't matter which way you go," said the Cat.

Alice's Adventures in Wonderland
Lewis Carroll (1920, p. 81)

Acknowledgments

I wish to give special thanks to Linda Bump, the developmental editor at Human Kinetics. Her positive attitude and constructive feedback were much appreciated. I would also like to give honorable mention to Eleonora, Melba, Rose, and Ruby for their unselfish efforts at the word processor. Finally, and most importantly, I would like to dedicate this book to my wife and best friend Nancy. Thanks for always being there when I needed you.

Chapter 1
Coaching Administration

For most of us, whether we recognize it or not, administration plays a major role in our everyday lives. Almost all the actions we perform on a given day have been predetermined by some form of administration. For example, the grocery store manager determines our food prices, the school principal determines the students' code of conduct, the government determines our taxes, and so on. Whether we are planning our monthly budgets, organizing household chores, interacting with people at work, or simply sitting in an easy chair evaluating our day, we are certainly engaging in specific forms of administrative behavior.

Although we all perform administrative tasks every day, proficiency in these tasks varies from one person to another. Certain individuals always seem to be on top of things, while others seem overwhelmed. Some people seem exceptionally organized, others completely disorganized. Some seem always to be running around in a panic, while others appear completely in control. More than likely, the major difference between these types of people lies in their relative administrative skills. Stated another way, some individuals are better than others at efficiently planning, organizing, leading, and controlling their available resources to complete desired tasks. In essence, these processes are what we mean by the term *administration*. Throughout this *Coaches Guide*, administration is defined as the process you use to guide your program toward some goal. Because administration plays such an important role in successful coaching, let's look at what the area has to offer you in your efforts to improve your coaching effectiveness.

By now your past experiences have shown you that coaching is a diverse subject area requiring competence in a wide variety of skills. For example, as a coach you must have the ability to plan short- and long-term events and organize your team's efforts toward its goals. You must have the ability to communicate with a wide spectrum of people ranging from top-level sport administrators to individual athletes. And you must be able to budget the financial and human resources available to your program. In addition to possessing these individual skills, you must know how to use them in the proper combination to produce the best possible coaching results. For example, it would do you little good to have all the technical expertise in the world if you didn't know how to communicate it to your athletes. Similarly, as a coach, you

would probably fail to reach your potential if you approached coaching in a haphazard, disorganized fashion. Because of the many factors involved in being a successful coach, developing appropriate administrative skills is necessary to allow you to maximize your coaching effectiveness.

Far too often, we coaches find ourselves in the position of having to react to a situation as it occurs. This undesirable coaching technique, known as *management by crisis*, forces us to deal with a situation that is already beyond our control. This *Guide* is designed to help you approach coaching and administering your sport program more scientifically. The *Coaches Guide to Sport Administration* provides you with the necessary tools to approach your coaching in an organized fashion.

ESSENTIAL SKILLS OF A COACH

It has already been pointed out that coaching requires a great variety of specific skills. In general, these skills can be classified as technical, human, and conceptual skills. Let's take a look at some examples from each of these categories.

Technical Skills

Skills involving your understanding of and proficiency in a specific kind of activity, particularly one involving methods, processes, procedures, and techniques, are termed *technical skills*. Some of the more common technical skills you are involved with in coaching include setting goals, making budgets, organizing practice plans, running successful team meetings, and developing a yearly training program. Technical knowledge of the actual sport skills in your program, including the ability to detect errors, is another example of a related technical skill.

Though coaches may often develop these skills to a certain extent by trial and error, it obviously makes more sense to learn the proper methods in the first place. This approach is both faster and more efficient. Because it would be impossible for any one text to cover all of the technical skills involved in

coaching, the *Coaches Guide to Sport Administration* focuses specifically on the development of *technical administrative skills*, such as planning, organizing, leading, and controlling. Once you have mastered these techniques, you will be well on your way to improving your coaching effectiveness.

Human Skills

Your ability to get along with other people, motivate them, and work well with them in the sporting environment relies on *human skills*. These skills are very important in maintaining team harmony, bringing about needed change, and managing potential conflict situations. No matter how great your technical skills are, you also must have the ability to work closely with your athletes. Coaching, after all, really boils down to working with people.

Developing the proper human skills, then, is a very important ingredient in becoming a successful coach. For this reason, the *Coaches Guide* focuses a substantial amount of material on techniques for developing your interpersonal skills. The *Coaches Guide to Sport Psychology* (Martens, 1987) provides excellent information aimed at developing your communication skills. This *Guide* goes one step further to complement your newly developed communication skills by providing you with interpersonal techniques focused on bringing about needed change and handling conflict situations. Improving your human skills will undoubtedly improve your overall coaching performance.

Conceptual Skills

Your ability to recognize how the various coaching functions depend on one another and how changes in one aspect affect all the others is a conceptual skill. An example of this is the ability to see how the various aspects of mental preparation interrelate with physiological preparation to produce a peak performance. With this understanding, you would then incorporate mental training into your yearly practice plan. Mental training is also discussed in the *Coaches Guide to Sport Psychology* (Martens, 1987).

An additional example from the coaching environment is the ability to see how human skills combine with technical skills to produce an optimal situation for your athletes' development. Even though as a coach you may be providing excellent technical advice, the manner in which you relate to the athlete undoubtedly affects the overall success of the coaching situation. Further examples of conceptual skills will become obvious as we examine the underlying processes of coaching administration.

Developing Your Skills

This *Coaches Guide* focuses on the development of technical, human, and conceptual skills as they relate to sport administration. By developing your skills, you will increase your efficiency and your enjoyment of coaching.

THE UNDERLYING PROCESS OF COACHING ADMINISTRATION

We have already defined coaching administration as the process you use to guide your program toward some goal. The term *process* refers to the *planning, organizing, leading,* and *controlling* that takes place to accomplish

your coaching objectives. Let's take a brief look at what is involved in each of these four processes, and see how they can help us become better coaches.

Planning

You are engaging in planning when you do such things as put together your season's game schedule, develop your yearly training program, formulate your season's goals, make the necessary arrangements for road trips, and so on. *Planning* is determining in advance what is to be done, how it is to be done, and who is going to do it. It involves setting objectives as well as making day-to-day decisions on how these objectives can best be achieved. Finally, planning requires you to establish objectives and standards that can be used to determine whether you are achieving your desired coaching goals.

Planning is one of the most important (and often most neglected) functions of any successful coach. Although we all engage in planning activities from time to time, we often fail to utilize several basic planning guidelines that make our efforts much more rewarding. For this reason, a variety of planning techniques are examined in chapter 2. Each of these suggestions will help you focus your program and plan a successful, enjoyable season.

Organizing

Organizing involves establishing relationships between the activities to be performed, the people who will perform them, and the physical factors that are required to accomplish your goals. Regardless of the level of sport at which you are coaching, it is very important that you learn to organize clear-cut responsibilities among the players, coaching staff, and parents. This results in more efficient use of time and human resources. Once this has been done, the remainder of your efforts can be focused exclusively on the *bottom line* of coaching—developing each athlete's potential. At other times in your coaching career, you may be required to set up fund-raising events or organize tournament draws. Each of these situations requires specific knowledge if you are to do the best job possible. Keeping this in mind, chapters 3, 4, and 5 provide you with a variety of organizational tools to make your job as a coach much easier.

Leading

In the *leadership* function, you are primarily involved in guiding and supervising your athletes. Being a leader involves maintaining effective working relationships with sport administrators, parents, athletes, and fellow coaches on a daily basis. Some of the tasks you are required to perform include motivating athletes, developing effective communication, bringing about needed change, and handling conflicts. As with most things in life, there are right ways and wrong ways to accomplish each of these tasks. Chapter 6 provides a wide range of techniques that will greatly improve your overall leadership ability in each of these coaching situations. The end result, of course, is that you will become a much more effective leader, and consequently a much more effective coach.

Controlling

The final link in the functional chain of coaching administration is control. Stated simply, it involves checking on all phases of your program to see if things are going as planned. You will recall that in the planning phase you set your overall objectives and determined how they would be evaluated. In the control phase, you actually perform a three-step evaluation. First you measure the actual performance results. Next you compare those results to the objectives you developed in the planning phase. Finally, when you encounter significant deviations from your initial objectives, you take some form of corrective action.

In chapter 7, the information required to develop an effective control system for your sport is presented. This in turn provides you with a workable approach to evaluating your season's objectives. Finally, chapter 7 outlines the procedure for zero-base budgeting. This allows you to control your financial resources more effectively.

THE ONGOING PROCESS OF COACHING ADMINISTRATION

Figure 1.1 illustrates the relationships involved in the ongoing process of coaching administration. It also represents a working blueprint for developing your administrative coaching skills.

We defined coaching administration as a process of planning, organizing, leading, and controlling. Obviously, each of these functions requires decisions, so any study of coaching administration must include the development of decision-making skills, which is discussed in chapter 8. These are the components, then, that make up the major sections of this *Coaches Guide*. By developing the administrative skills presented in this text, you will be well on your way to becoming a more efficient and more successful coach.

SUMMARY AND RECOMMENDATIONS

Three essential skills and four basic processes in coaching administration were previewed. The following chapters provide you with a variety of tools to help you develop the administrative skills necessary to become a more successful coach. Each of the following chapters begins by introducing you to the importance of the chapter's topic from a coaching standpoint and gives specific examples of how you can use the administrative technique in your coaching situation. Finally, each chapter closes with specific recommendations that will aid you in performing your coaching duties.

Consider the following recommendations based on the importance of good administrative techniques:

1. Because of the multitude of factors involved in successful coaching, strive to develop administrative skills that will help you focus your coaching efforts. This in turn will greatly enhance your coaching effectiveness.
2. By developing these skills, you will find yourself less frequently in *management-by-crisis* situations. A well-

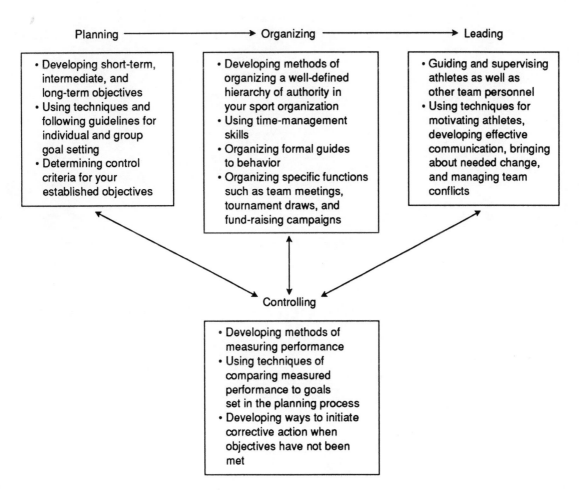

Figure 1.1. The ongoing process of coaching administration.

planned and organized sport program eliminates many of the problems that invariably surface in the coaching environment. This lack of crisis orientation, in turn, allows you to focus your attention solely upon developing your athletes' potential.

Chapter 2
Planning for Better Coaching

The new season is only a month away. Already you are looking forward to the first practice and the opportunity to work with your athletes. You feel you are ready, but have you considered

- what administrative duties must be completed before the season gets under way;
- what administrative duties will have to be performed throughout the season;
- what your personal coaching goals, priorities, and expectations are;
- what your athletes' goals, priorities, and expectations might be; and
- what the team's goals, priorities, and strategies should be?

A TALE OF TWO COACHES

Though every coach is involved in planning, the extent and effectiveness of this planning obviously varies from one person to the next. To illustrate this point, let's meet two coaches who approach planning from different perspectives.

Coach Ralph

Ralph is beginning his 2nd year as coach of the Beeman Blues peewee hockey team. One morning only 2 weeks before the opening game of the season, Ralph decides it is time to call the first team meeting. Because he is already late for work, he asks his wife to place an ad in the community paper announcing the first team meeting, with a full dress practice to follow. His wife asks the date and time of this session; Ralph reflects for a moment, then responds, "8:00 Sunday morning." Ralph assumes that just like last year, that time is best to schedule practice.

When Ralph arrives at the arena 15 minutes early, he is surprised to see the university hockey team fully dressed and waiting to get on the ice. When two of his returning players ask him what is going on, Ralph replies that there must be some sort of mistake, and storms off to find the facility manager. When he finally locates the individual responsible for ice bookings, he demands an explanation as to why the university team is expecting to use his ice time. After all, Ralph explains, "We practiced at this time every Sunday last year, so I assumed you booked us for this year as well." Ralph is informed that bookings are recorded on a first-come, first-serve basis, and he will have to schedule another time for his team. Fortunately, there is an opening from 9:00 to 10:00 A.M. each Sunday, so Ralph grudgingly makes the new arrangements. He then goes to inform his team of the "misunderstanding" and suggests that they watch the big guys play for the next half hour. After that, they will start the team meeting in one of the dressing rooms.

With the team finally assembled, some of the players point out that they will not be able to stay for the full practice because their parents are coming to pick them up at 9:30. At this point, somewhat rattled by the morning's events, Ralph's initial talk comes across as completely disorganized, leaving many of the players wondering what he really said. The following dialogue between Ralph and last year's captain does nothing to improve the situation:

Captain: Hey, Coach, what do you think we have to do to improve our league record this year?

Coach: Well, to be honest with you, Randy, I haven't given it much thought yet. Let's wait until we see how the team looks after the first few practices.

Captain: But you must have some ideas, don't you, Coach?

Coach: Well, yes, I guess we will all have to try harder.

Captain: But we tried as hard as we could last year, Coach.

Coach: Well, it wasn't hard enough. Anyway, time's wasting. Let's hit the ice.

Once on the ice, Ralph instructs his athletes to skate around until they are warmed up. Then, because he has neglected to put together a practice plan, he allows his team to scrimmage until the buzzer signals the end to the first practice. At this point, Ralph reminds the remaining players that the team will meet again next Sunday at 9:00 A.M.

Four weeks later, three of his best players drop out, complaining that they are tired of doing the same old thing every practice.

Coach Bob

Across town, Bob is also beginning his second season of coaching youth hockey. Exactly one month prior to the first league game, Bob places an ad in the community paper announcing the first practice for the Beeman Bullets, a crosstown rival of the Blues. He also mails a form letter to each of last year's returning players, in which he informs the boys of the place and time of their first practice (he has already reserved ice time). He also stresses the importance of each individual's attendance, pointing out that an exhibition game has been arranged as a tune-up the week before their league opener. He also asks each player to arrive 15 minutes before ice time for a short team meeting.

When practice day arrives, all the players show up precisely on time. Bob assembles the boys in the team's dressing room for the initial team meeting. After some introductory comments, the coach confirms the team's practice times through the end of the season. He also briefly goes over the league schedule and tells the players he will provide a photocopy of the schedule after practice. Bob encourages each player to show his parents the schedule because he will be contacting each family in the next week to inquire about the best times for their cooperation in driving to one of the league away games. Before Bob has a chance to continue, one of the players asks the inevitable question, and the ensuing dialogue is as follows:

Player: What are we going to do to improve our league record this year, Coach?

Coach: Well, I do have some ideas, and I'd like to go over them with you. But I also think you guys must have some good suggestions, too.

Player: Gee, I don't know . . .

Coach: Well, we aren't going to be able to solve all our problems today, so I'd like to suggest that we spend about 10 minutes at the end of each practice sharing our ideas about how to improve the team, starting next week. In the meantime, I want all you guys to give some thought as to how we can be even better this year. We will start going over our ideas next Sunday.

Player: You mean you're really going to let us help you plan our season? That sounds great.

Coach: Right. We'll set our goals together, then see how many of them we can make come true.

Once on the ice, Bob takes his players through a four-stage workout, as outlined on his practice plan. He starts off with 10 minutes of warm-up exercise followed by 20 to 30 minutes of drills combining skating skills with aerobic training. Next, he holds a 20-minute scrimmage, and concludes with a 10-minute cool-down period.

About a month later, Bob's players are showing marked improvement from that initial practice.

Planning and Effective Coaching

What is it that sets Ralph and Bob apart in the previous two examples? Obviously it is the willingness and ability to plan effectively for the upcoming season. You will recall that in chapter 1, planning was defined as determining in advance what is to be done, how it is to be done, and who is going to do it. Planning is like a cook's recipe or a motorist's road map—it results in a plotted-out course of where to go and how to get there.

Ralph, for example, did not take the time to plan in advance for such things as establishing a date for the first team meeting or booking practice time. He also showed poor planning in terms of what his athletes needed to further develop their skills in the upcoming season, or how he was actually going to go about developing these skills. As a result, the initial team meeting and practice came across as completely disorganized. This pattern obviously continued, as witnessed by the fact that three of Ralph's best players dropped out, complaining of a lack of direction in their practices.

Bob, on the other hand, had the foresight to thoroughly plan the same details overlooked by Ralph. His athletes were notified well in advance of the initial team meeting and practice, resulting in a favorable first session. Bob also appeared to have thought about some season objectives for the team as well as individual players' development. He followed a carefully developed practice plan. As a result of his planning efforts, his athletes showed marked improvement in only the first month of play.

Ralph and Bob certainly differed in terms of their approach to planning the initial team meeting. Their examples, as well as the experiences of many other coaches I interviewed, highlight the following tips for planning your initial team meeting:

- Notify your athletes of the meeting well in advance and make sure you provide the necessary details regarding the specific purpose of the team meeting, as well as the date, time, and place.
- Make sure you tell those people coming to the meeting exactly what they will be required to do and whether they need to bring anything.

- Try to get some idea of how many people are going to attend the first meeting. This is best accomplished by either making phone calls or enclosing return slips with the original notice.
- If you are dealing with young athletes, it is a good idea to set aside some time for talking with parents, perhaps during a parent orientation program. Another way this can be accomplished is by sending parents a letter introducing yourself and your coaching philosophy.
- Plan some time for discussing individual and group goal setting, as well as the means by which this will be accomplished.
- Be prepared to offer suggestions about what equipment athletes should purchase.
- Be prepared to field some questions on preseason training as well as goals or strategies for the upcoming season.
- Allow plenty of time to answer questions. This shows your athletes that you care about their individual concerns. It also helps create a relaxed atmosphere for future team meetings.

Observing these guidelines for conducting the initial team meeting will greatly improve your initial performance with your athletes. Other tips regarding preseason planning are provided in the *Coaches Guide to Time Management* (Kozoll, 1985), *Coaches Guide to Teaching Sport Skills* (Christina & Corcos, 1988), *Coaching Young Athletes* (Martens, Christina, Harvey, & Sharkey, 1981), and *Successful Coaching* (Martens, 1990). Let's turn our attention to the planning process and see how it can improve your coaching effectiveness.

FIVE STEPS IN SUCCESSFUL PLANNING FOR COACHES

The process of planning by an effective coach should encompass the following successive stages:

- Setting overall objectives
- Setting specific goals
- Identifying specific courses of action (strategies) to meet these goals

- Developing specific standards of performance for evaluating progress toward meeting objectives
- Evaluating progress

Let's look at each of these successful planning stages in detail and see how they can make us more effective coaches.

Step 1: Setting Overall Objectives

The first step in the planning process is to identify your overall objectives for the season. Overall objectives reflect your philosophy and your reasons for being involved in sport. Stated another way, these overall objectives are general statements about what you want out of the season. You can define your own overall objectives by responding to the following questions:

- What do you want your athletes to get out of this year's sport experience?
- What are the season's priorities?
- What is the relative importance of fun, fitness development, skill development, social development, and sportsmanship?

Remember, overall objectives are *general* statements you make about desired outcomes for your season. Here are two examples of overall objectives in their stated form:

- To provide my athletes with the opportunity to further develop their skills, learn how to get along with their teammates, and have fun in the process.
- To remember that my athletes are always more important than the results of any contest.

Step 2: Setting Specific Goals

Specific goals are overall objectives that have been further developed. Specific goals lead to behaviors that are *observable, measurable,* and *achievable.* Because these three criteria are of utmost importance in setting specific goals, let's take a closer look at what each has to offer the serious coach.

When we talk about sport behavior, we are referring to the things that our athletes do. They run, shoot basketballs, swing baseball bats, and kick soccer balls. Those actions are observable and measurable. Other features of athletes do not fall within these boundaries. Personality traits, attitudes, and understanding are characteristics that cannot be directly observed or measured.

When setting specific goals, always make sure they are observable and measurable. Consider our first overall objective in Step 1. It is of little value to set such a specific goal as, "The athlete will understand how to execute an overhand volleyball serve" in an attempt to attain that objective. In this case, we have no way of observing or measuring if the desired understanding has actually taken place. On the other hand, if our specific goal is stated as, "The athlete will be able to successfully deliver an overhand volleyball serve into a designated area," we can directly observe and measure if the desired learning actually occurs. You will be able to gauge your coaching effectiveness only if you set specific goals that are observable and measurable.

The third criterion for setting specific goals dictates that these goals be achievable. To set achievable specific goals, you must first consider your athletes' needs, the physical resources available, and the sport resources available in your particular circumstances. As a coach, it is important to remember that athletes' needs are directly related to their levels of physical development, skill, fitness, experience in competition, and motivation. Because different athletes obviously have different levels of development in each of these areas, the coach must take these individual differences into account when developing specific goals.

If you fail to do this, you may set a goal that is beyond the reach of your athletes. This can be a serious problem, because it often results in loss of motivation. The key thing to keep in mind when setting an achievable goal is that the goal must be both challenging and attainable. This combination has been found to maximize athlete motivation. In our previous example of a specific goal relating to the overhand volleyball serve, the coach determined that the athletes' skill level was appropriate for the stated goal. If this had not been the case, the goal would not have been achievable. You can learn to set challenging yet realistic goals. Get to know your athletes! Or investigate the use of discrepancy scores (Bump, 1989).

Another factor to consider in setting achievable goals involves physical resources. Examples of physical resources are facilities, equipment, and space. The extent of an athlete's progress is largely determined by these factors. Before planning specific goals, you must take into account the quantity, quality, accessibility, and safety of these physical resources.

A final aid in developing specific goals is the availability of sport resource material. For example, developmental guides, progress charts, teaching progressions, films, and technical manuals may be valuable in helping you create observable, measurable, and attainable goals.

Only when athlete needs, physical resources, and sport resources have been carefully considered is it possible to proceed with the planning process. With this information you will be able to develop specific goals that are observable, measurable, and achievable.

Step 3: Identifying Specific Courses of Action

This step merely asks you to identify possible ways of attaining the goals set in the previous stages. It requires you to formulate alternate courses of action to meet your goals. Examples that you might consider in the case of teaching your athletes a technical skill are (a) following the normal teaching progressions outlined in the technical manual; (b) using regular and slow-motion films that demonstrate the proper technique; (c) demonstrating the proper technique yourself; and (d) allowing a great deal of practice time. The challenge left to you is to select which alternative is the best solution.

Step 4: Developing Specific Standards for Evaluation

In this step, you are asked to determine standards that must be attained for you to define progress toward the stated goal as acceptable. In Step 2, when we discussed how to develop specific goals, I stressed that goals must be observable, measurable, and achievable. You also saw that for this to be possible, you must consider the athlete's needs, the physical resources, and the sport resources available in your particular situation. Once all these factors have been considered, you can determine the standard of performance that you feel is acceptable at any given time. When this has been done, you are ready to write your specific performance and nonperformance goals.

Writing Specific Performance Goals

There are four established elements in writing specific performance goals.

- State exactly what it is that you want (e.g., the athlete will learn the slice serve in tennis).
- Describe the desired end product or behavior that you want (e.g., the athlete will be able to perform a good and legal slice serve in practices and games).
- State the conditions of performance (e.g., the athlete will use a regulation racquet from the baseline without foot-faulting).
- Decide the current criteria of acceptable performance. This refers to the specific goal for the day (e.g., the athlete will be able to legally slice-serve 6 out of 10 balls into the proper court at the end of the practice using a regulation racquet).

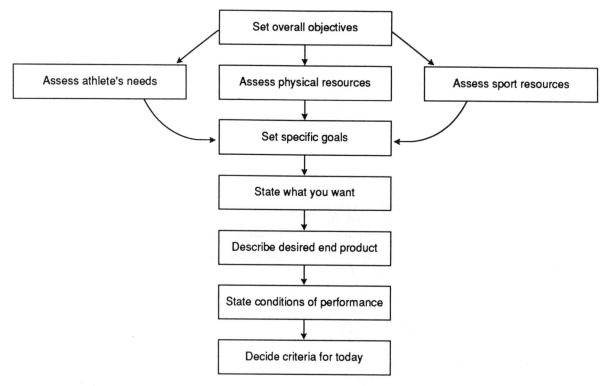

Figure 2.1. Stages in writing specific performance objectives.

The process of writing specific performance objectives can best be summarized by the chart shown in Figure 2.1.

Two examples of specific performance goals are provided below:

- In a simulated hockey game situation, each defenseman should be able to make 6 out of 10 slap shots on net at the end of today's practice.
- At the end of today's softball practice, each player should be able to bunt fairly, using the proper technique, 6 out of 10 pitches thrown within the strike zone.

Writing Specific Nonperformance Goals

Not all goals are performance-related; some are concerned with attitudes and sportsmanship. It is just as important to write specific objectives for these desired end products as for performance goals. Once again, it is important to state the goals in observable, measurable, and achievable terms. The following are some examples of specific, non-performance-related goals:

- To have my records show a 50% reduction over last season in the number of practices my players miss.

- To reduce my team's overall penalty minutes statistics by at least 20%.

It is important to note that your coaching effectiveness can be greatly improved if you write specific goals that are observable, measurable, and achievable. By so doing, you will be providing direction and criteria for evaluating the progress your athlete or team is making.

Step 5: Evaluating Progress

The last step in the planning process involves the actual evaluation. Because you have already established goals that are directly measurable, all that remains is to determine if the specific standards have been met. To evaluate the specific performance goals cited in Step 4, you would set up your practice situation so that you could actually measure or count the number of shots on net recorded by the defenseman, or the number of fair bunts executed by the softball players.

If the determined standards are not met, corrective action is required. This corrective action can take one of three different forms: First, you may need to restate your goal—it might not have been specific enough to be adequately measured or improved. For example, if the coach in the hockey example had stated the objective as "to improve the defenseman's shooting accuracy," it might be difficult to monitor because players could use both wrist shots and slap shots. When the actual measurement or evaluation takes place, the players may utilize a preponderance of wrist shots and hence not meet the intention of your established standard—improving slap shots. It is therefore important to be specific in terms of the skill you wish to improve.

Second, you could go back and try one of the alternate coaching strategies developed in Step 3. This is often effective because some athletes learn better from one type of coaching technique than from others. For example, some individuals have to see the technique performed correctly before they are able to successfully execute the skill. These athletes especially benefit from viewing regular and slow-motion films of the technique. Other athletes respond especially well to verbal explanations. Whatever the case, if the established standard is not met, it is advisable to utilize an alternate strategy.

Third, it is sometimes best to redefine your standards of performance so that they are attainable. Although utilizing different strategies and different combinations of strategies usually gets you back on track, sometimes even this doesn't work. Sometimes, with all good intentions, we set standards of performance that are too high or too unrealistic. When this is the case, it is advisable to take another look at your determined standards of performance. This is a very important point because research has shown that realistic goals lead to increased motivation, whereas unrealistic goals have the opposite effect.

When standards of performance are not met, the wise coach goes back and examines previous steps to determine why sufficient progress is not being achieved. As a result, the five steps in planning should represent an ongoing process as illustrated in Figure 2.2.

The major implication from Figure 2.2 is that evaluating progress is both the final step of one practice and the first step to creating the next. By following this approach, you will continue to develop your coaching effectiveness.

PUTTING IT ALL TOGETHER

The following planning tool will help you put the five stages of planning together into a workable coaching blueprint. I use a specific volleyball example here, but keep in mind that individual coaches must develop their own goal-setting blueprint based on their overall objectives as well as each team's specific needs. You will be given the opportunity to develop your own blueprint in the *Study Guide*. Using a guide similar to the volleyball worksheet on page 14 will help you build a more successful season for your athletes.

OTHER FACTORS TO CONSIDER IN PLANNING

Up to this point, we have concentrated exclusively on goal setting as performed by the coach for a specific practice or game. Now let's focus on group goal setting as well as the development of short-term, intermediate, and long-term goals. Both types of goal setting are valuable in improving your coaching effectiveness.

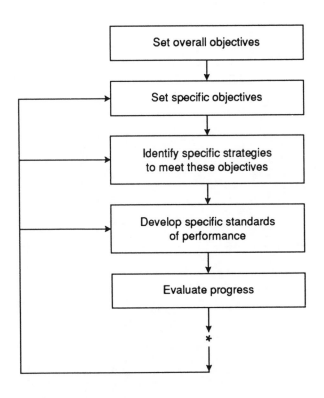

*If standards are not met, reevaluate

Figure 2.2. The ongoing planning process.

Volleyball Planning and Goal-Setting Worksheet

Step 1 Setting overall objectives	Step 2 Setting specific goals	Step 3 Identifying strategies to meet specific goals	Step 4 Developing standards of performance	Step 5 Evaluating progress
To further develop volleyball skill levels in my athletes.	I want my players to show improved service reception this year.	Utilize technical manuals—go back to basics. Spend more time on service reception drills at each practice session. Utilize a performance information chart in a simulated game situation at the conclusion of each practice.	In a simulated game situation at the end of this month, I want 25% of the service receptions going to the designated setter.	Record this statistic in the simulated game situation at the end of the month and compare it with the standard of performance set in Step 4.
	I want my team to learn completely the ''6-player-up'' defense.	Use films and film clips of teams that successfully use this system. Walk through system each practice. Record practices on videotape to allow analysis and discussion.	In a simulated game situation at the end of this week, I want no more than three positional errors for a complete team rotation.	Measure the number of positional errors and compare to Step 4.
To teach my players how to get along with others and have fun in the process.	I would like to see a reduction in the number of missed practices over the course of the year.	Introduce more variety into my practice sessions. Use simulation training. Set up more social events (e.g., going out for pizza and pop).	This year, I want to see a 50% reduction over last year in the number of practices missed.	Take attendance over the course of the season, tabulate absences, and compare them with last year's figures.

Group Goal Setting

Research (Botterill, 1979) has shown that a simple process of team goal setting with athletes can

- clarify issues and help reduce confusion or misunderstanding regarding team goals, priorities, and expectations;
- determine if the coach's goals and priorities are in line with those of the athletes;
- serve as an effective motivational and leadership technique because athlete involvement leads to commitment;
- heighten your credibility as a coach by showing the athletes that you are interested in helping them achieve their goals;
- help teach athletes to make their own decisions and accept responsibility for their own actions;
- help foster self-discipline and self-reliance in your players; and
- help foster communication between coaches and athletes.

Please review the section on individualized goal setting outlined in the *Coaches Guide to Sport Psychology* (Martens, 1987). You can adapt the techniques described and integrate them into a team framework.

Short-Term, Intermediate, and Long-Term Plans

Another consideration in the planning process involves establishing short-term, intermediate, and long-term plans. Generally speaking, short-term plans cover a period of 1 month or less; intermediate plans cover up to 1 year; and long-term plans range from 1 to 4 years. Let's look at some examples of each type of planning from the coaching environment. Examples of short-term plans include monthly practice schedules, weekly plans, and daily practice plans. Intermediate plans involve the yearly competition schedule, the yearly training program, practice planning, and budget preparation for the current fiscal year. You might also include plans for individual stages of development for each athlete or the entire team, linking the current year to the long-term plans. One example from the track environment would be a decrease in the time for the mile run over the course of the year, along with increases in the level of competition from year to year. Following this example, long-term plans would involve development of each athlete to his or her maximal potential at the most appropriate time. Developing long-term plans almost invariably involves several years of preparation.

Upon first glance, you may feel this distinction seems to imply that intermediate and long-term plans increase in importance with the caliber of the athlete and the coach. On a more basic level, however, all coaches should develop intermediate and long-term plans to ensure that athletes continue participation and maintain a proper pace of development. These goals are not valuable just for elite athletes. If as a coach you are more concerned with immediate results, adequate concentration on basic skill development might be sacrificed for short-term gains. But in the final analysis, such a practice limits the athlete's ultimate potential as well as your effectiveness as a coach. Short-sightedness also adds to the risk of increasing dropouts if you try to push your athletes too far too fast.

In summary, the development of short-term, intermediate, and long-term plans is an important link in the development of your overall coaching effectiveness. Only coaches who utilize all three types of plans will help their athletes reach their maximal potential.

PLANNING DURING THE OFF-SEASON

Coaches must also consider off-season responsibilities in the planning process. The successful coach immediately recognizes that his or her responsibilities do not end with the competitive season. The off-season represents an important time that can be used to your coaching advantage. Let's take a few minutes to consider what functions you can perform during this period to improve your coaching effectiveness.

Evaluation

Perhaps the first thing you should do at the conclusion of the season is evaluate the past year's performance. Earlier in this chapter,

you learned the five steps in successful planning for coaches. The last step in this process involved evaluating progress. Use the same evaluation procedure at the conclusion of the season to determine whether specific goals have been met. Review the overall goals and objectives you established in the planning process and determine if these goals were indeed accomplished. If they were, start thinking about new goals for next year. If your original goals were not achieved, try to determine why not, and revise your goals for next year accordingly. Remember, it is never too early to start planning for next year.

Equipment

A second off-season responsibility involves taking inventory of your equipment and planning your purchases for next season. Planning for the purchase and care of equipment is one of the coach's or athletic administrator's most important jobs. When athletes are forced to use inadequate or insufficient equipment, your desired performance goals will seldom be attained. It is your responsibility to provide quality equipment for every aspect of your

sport program. The importance of proper equipment purchases dictates adherence to a series of fundamental buying principles (Voltmer, Esslinger, McCue, & Tillman, 1979). To familiarize you with these recommendations, let's review the guidelines in terms of their potential to improve your purchasing effectiveness.

Standardization of Equipment

Most coaches and athletic directors prefer to purchase equipment of a particular color, style, and type that can be maintained over several years. This allows you to replace the equipment in mass or in several small orders. This practice is not only more economical; it also results in uniformity over a period of seasons. For example, if you purchase the same style and color of volleyball uniform over several years, you are free to replace only those portions that show excessive wear (e.g., the trunks). The same argument also holds for athletic equipment such as balance beams, basketball hoops, goalposts, golf clubs, and so on. Standardizing your equipment will make your organization appear more professional and will save money in the long term.

Buy Quality Merchandise

Most coaches and athletic directors agree that it is best to purchase the better grades of equipment. Although quality merchandise costs a bit more initially, it usually lasts longer and can be repaired more effectively. Far too many coaches fall into the trap of buying the least expensive equipment in an attempt to save the team money. This usually results in early replacement, which costs more in the long run. For example, if you buy 12 basketballs at the cheapest price and they last only 1 year, you will end up spending more money to replace them than you would have spent if you had purchased 12 quality balls with the durability to last several years. The least expensive item does not *always* represent the greatest overall savings. Intermediate and long-term planning must be utilized in effective equipment purchasing.

Order Early

There are several advantages to ordering your athletic equipment early. First of all, early ordering usually means early delivery. This is very important because it allows you to correct any shipping mistakes, make size adjustments, and order any additional items as necessary. A second advantage to early ordering is that it provides you with the opportunity to mark and store your equipment properly. By taking the time to store it properly, you ensure your equipment against damage from such factors as moisture, rodents, and sunlight. And early ordering usually results in better craftsmanship by unhurried workers. To benefit from all these advantages, order your equipment as early as possible.

Consider Your Program's Interests

Know what equipment and supplies you need and order only from the dealer with the best price and quality combination. Unfortunately, it is common for sporting equipment dealers to offer gifts to coaches and sport administrators to secure their business. A set of golf clubs, a pair of your favorite running shoes, or that professional-looking tennis racquet may be offered as compensation for a favorable decision to purchase with that specific dealer. Always decline such gifts on the grounds of professional ethics. Equipment should be purchased with the sport organization's best interests, not your own, in mind.

Purchase From Reputable Companies

One of the best ways to choose an equipment supplier is to talk to other coaches and sport administrators. Retailers' reputations usually precede them. By taking the time to ask around, you can quickly determine the suppliers with the best (and worst!) reputations. This simple process can go a long way in eliminating the trial-and-error problems that invariably accompany equipment purchases.

Purchase From Local Dealers Whenever Possible

Always try to give preference to local dealers, provided that their equipment is of equal quality at competitive prices. I recommend this policy because local dealers can usually provide better and faster service within the community. Because they are a hometown company, they are greatly concerned with their reputation in the community. They are also likely to offer better prices and services to your sport organization.

Equipment Wrap-Up

One final word about equipment concerns its proper care. Because the materials from which equipment is made vary so drastically (e.g., wood, rubber, leather, fabrics, metal, among others), there can be no single policy regarding care of equipment. As such, your best approach is to follow manufacturers' guidelines. Their procedures were developed to ensure maximum equipment life and playability.

By observing these simple guidelines, you will minimize any problems with your equipment purchases. By planning early, you can purchase early. This allows you to remedy any equipment problems well in advance of the new season.

Budget

The off-season is also the time to start thinking about next year's budget. I deal exclusively with budgeting in chapter 7. For now, it is sufficient to remember to include this important function in the off-season. Budgeting is fast becoming a major limiting factor to athletic performance, so you must take this responsibility seriously.

Scheduling

Another important off-season responsibility involves setting up next year's schedule, both regular-season and exhibition competitions. Usually, this function entails initiating correspondence with other coaches and athletic directors and results in written agreements or contracts between the participating teams outlining the dates, places, and times of competition. In large sport organizations, the conditions can become far more complex, involving such factors as compensation, gate receipts, penalties for no-shows, and so on.

A complete analysis of the legalities of contracts is beyond the scope of this book. Interested readers are encouraged to examine this issue in more depth in Jensen (1983). For most coaches, however, a formal schedule is usually provided by the league administrator. When this is the case, your responsibility is limited to arranging exhibition contests with interested competitors.

Facility Rental

We saw earlier in this chapter how Coach Ralph neglected to arrange for use of the ice rink and the problems that later resulted. It is a good policy to book your facility for both practices and competitions as early as possible. This will prevent serious disappointments later. Furthermore, if you have difficulty securing space, you will have ample time to investigate alternatives.

Correspondence

One final off-season responsibility for coaches involves follow-up letters to the athletes and their parents, thanking them for their involvement during the season. A letter of this nature is a nice touch—it adds a personal dimension to the program. You may also find it results in greater parental support of your program. In addition, this letter can be used to reinforce your philosophy of coaching.

SUMMARY AND RECOMMENDATIONS

These words were printed on a sugar wrapper once served with my coffee: "In failing to plan, we are planning to fail." Although perhaps a bit clichéd, the statement calls to mind the experience that is far too prevalent among coaches—poor results due to poor planning. As you consider the role that planning plays in making you a better coach, remember the following recommendations:

1. The willingness and ability to plan effectively for the upcoming season is a major factor that distinguishes successful coaches from unsuccessful ones.
2. Make sure you have carefully planned your initial team meeting. Starting the season in a planned and organized fashion helps set a positive tone for the upcoming year.
3. The first step in the planning process is to identify your overall objectives for the season. These objectives should reflect your philosophy and, I hope, the ACEP philosophy of *Athletes First, Winning Second*.
4. Once you have established your overall objectives, it is important to develop and write down specific goals that are observable, measurable, and achievable.
5. Consider the short-term, intermediate, and long-term goals for your program.
6. Use the off-season to plan wisely for future seasons.

Chapter 3
Organizing for Success

In chapter 1, organizing was portrayed as establishing relationships between the activities to be performed, the people to perform them, and the physical factors that are required to accomplish your goals. For most coaches, time is the first thing that must be organized. The *Coaches Guide to Time Management* (Kozoll, 1985) provides excellent information aimed at developing your ability to effectively organize your valuable time. This chapter provides additional organizational practices to further develop your coaching effectiveness.

ORGANIZATIONAL CASE STUDIES

To illustrate the importance of organizational ability, let's focus our attention on four coaches who could really use some help in improving their organization skills. Although each personnel problem we will encounter is different, the use of proper organizational tech-

niques would eliminate occurrences of this nature.

Do-It-All Dora

For the past 10 years, Dora has been head coach of the varsity girls' basketball team. Basketball was always Dora's first love. Having played point guard at college, she enjoys being involved in the sport as a coach.

Four years ago, due to a staff vacancy, Dora was promoted to physical education department head. She maintained all her regular teaching and coaching duties, but also vowed to spend whatever time was needed to increase intramural participation because she saw the faltering program as a major priority. When she assumed the department headship, Jim, a new staff member, volunteered his services as assistant basketball coach, suggesting that this would help alleviate some of her responsibility for the team's success. Jim pointed out that he had played the post position in college and therefore could devote his attention to working with the "big" players. Although post play had faltered during the past couple of years, Dora declined Jim's offer, feeling the team was her sole responsibility. In the 4 years since, Dora's team has fallen out of contention for the league championship. Each year seems to bring a worse league record. Dora feels helpless in her efforts to pull the team out of its tailspin.

One Friday afternoon, as Dora was pondering the situation and feeling that things couldn't get much worse, she had a visit from the school principal, who informed her that he was receiving more and more complaints from students about the intramural program. The principal then told Dora that he was going to call a meeting with the entire physical education staff to discuss the problem and voice some other serious concerns.

Floundering Frank

There was no doubt in Frank's mind that this would be his best year yet. After 15 years of teaching high school, Frank accepted a job lecturing at a well-known college in his hometown. He also was named head coach of the women's varsity basketball team. Although Frank had never coached at this level of play, he felt his experience coaching the boys' high school team would provide an easy transition to the college basketball environment.

As it turned out, staff turnover required that the college athletic director also hire a new assistant coach. Although this was by no means an ideal situation, the AD was heartened by the fact that Betty had several years' experience as an assistant coach at another college. After Betty's appointment, the athletic director confided to her that, because this was Frank's first year coaching college ball, he would expect her to play a major role in team selection and early practice sessions. This, he felt, would make for an easier transition for Frank.

Unfortunately, the partnership did not work out as planned. When Frank accepted the position as head coach, he was told that he was solely responsible for all aspects of team development. He was also told that an assistant coach would be appointed to provide assistance as Frank requested. However, as head coach, Frank was expected to be the boss.

After the initial team tryouts and the first few practices, it became apparent that serious problems were developing. During team tryouts, Frank and Betty found themselves constantly disagreeing about player selection. Frank wanted a young team that could be developed over the next few years, but Betty wanted immediate results. Several unpleasant discussions took place before the team was finally selected.

At the first practice, Frank was annoyed when Betty showed up with a complete practice plan for the 2-hour session. Although Betty was acting in accordance with the athletic director's request, Frank saw this as a serious problem. He told Betty that he had his own practice plan and intended to use it. Even so, several times during the practice, Betty took command and ran some of her own drills.

Although both coaches acted professionally, it was obvious to the players that something was wrong. To further confound matters, last year's team captain pointed out that they followed a completely different practice format last season, and suggested that it be adopted this year as well. At this point, both Frank and Betty wondered why they ever accepted their new jobs. The team players also harbored serious doubts about leadership for the upcoming season. The next day, Frank resolved to meet with the athletic director to clear up the problem.

Trusting Tina

At a well-known high school across the country, a different type of organizational problem was evolving. Tina was in her 3rd year as coach of the varsity golf team, a squad composed of four players aged 17 to 19. Because golf is a tournament event, the teams must travel to the regional host site for competition. For this particular tournament, Tina drove the team in the school station wagon as she usually did and booked rooms at a reasonably priced motel. The tournament schedule allowed a practice round on Wednesday, followed by two tournament rounds on Thursday and Friday. For this reason, the team left Tuesday afternoon so that they would be well rested for Wednesday's round.

In her 2 years of coaching, Tina had never experienced problems with player conduct. This year, however, was a different story. After eating dinner together Tuesday night, the golfers asked Tina for permission to see an early movie at the local cinema, just four blocks from their motel. Tina immediately granted their request, but reminded the athletes to get a good night's sleep so they would be fresh for tomorrow's practice round. The players readily agreed.

At 10:00 P.M., after watching some television, Tina decided to look in on the team members to make sure they had returned early as promised. A brief room check indicated that the players had not come back to the motel. Tina returned to her room and proceeded to check the players' rooms every 15 minutes. After over 2 hours, at 12:30 A.M., Tina heard her athletes returning to their rooms. Their arrival was quite noisy, so she hurried out to the hallway and reminded the athletes that people were trying to sleep. She then asked them into her room for a brief talk. She expressed her disappointment that they did not return early as promised and suggested they turn in immediately.

Approximately a half hour later, Tina received a phone call from the motel manager, informing her that other guests were complaining about noise coming from her players' rooms. She was told they would have to leave if this boisterous behavior did not cease immediately.

Once again, Tina confronted her athletes and severely reprimanded their behavior. At one point, Tina thought she could smell alcohol, making her wonder if the players had been drinking. She tried to dismiss the idea but was left with a nagging sense of worry. What was going to happen next? She could not help wondering how she could have prevented this type of problem.

Personal Pete

In response to an ad in the local paper, Pete volunteered his services as coach of a city league baseball team. Coaching baseball was something Pete had always wanted to do. Now that he finally had his chance, he vowed to do the best job possible. So far, everything was running smoothly. Practices had been going on for almost 3 weeks, and the team was almost ready for its first league game the next week.

Coach Pete was very impressed with the attitude of one player in particular, a pitcher named Billy—by far the friendliest and most liked athlete on the squad. All was not a bed of roses, however; one of the best players on the team, Casey, was almost the exact opposite of Billy. Though he was an excellent pitcher, he was quite unpopular with his teammates. In addition, he often questioned coaching decisions in front of the other players. All in all, Pete found Casey very difficult to coach.

When it was finally time for the first game, Pete listed Billy as the starting pitcher, even though he was less talented than Casey. When Casey saw the lineup, he kicked over the bat rack and told Pete he was quitting the team. Although Coach Pete did everything he knew to try to discourage this type of behavior, he could not help but second-guess his decision. Without Casey, it was doubtful that the team could contend for the league championship.

THE KEY COMPONENTS OF ORGANIZATION

The preceding four examples have been used to illustrate what can happen when the classical cornerstones of organization are not followed. These cornerstones can be summarized as follows:

Principle 1: Formalize a division of labor and delegate responsibility.

Principle 2: Maintain a well-defined authority hierarchy.

Principle 3: Design formal guides to behavior.

Principle 4: Make administrative decisions based on merit, not on personalities.

Let's now look at each of these principles individually and see how their use could have prevented the problems experienced by the four coaches.

Divide and Delegate Responsibility

Most researchers agree that the division of labor, also known as specialization, tends to work for three main reasons:

- Physical limitations
- Knowledge limitations
- Time limitations

First, in highly sophisticated sports, physical limitations prevent one coach from performing all the activities; the coach cannot be in several locations at once. For example, it would be impossible for one baseball coach to handle all the coaching duties necessary for team development. For this reason, pitching coaches, batting coaches, first- and third-base coaches, and other specialty coaches are employed so that all aspects of the game can be developed. There is not enough time in a day for one coach to perform all these duties.

Earlier in the chapter, you read how Coach Dora found this out the hard way. It was impossible for her to fulfill the roles of head coach, department head, and intramural director. If she had accepted help when it was offered, chances are that all team members would have shown marked improvement instead of steady decline in performance. Because Dora had too many divergent roles, she was unable to devote the necessary attention to the guards, forwards, and posts. Therefore, it was impossible to produce a successful team.

Second, limitation of knowledge can be a serious constraint. If several of the sport tasks require large amounts of technical expertise, it may be impossible to find one coach who is familiar with all the activities involved.

This situation in itself could have been the main reason why Coach Dora's team fell out of league contention. Because of Dora's workload and refusal to accept help, she was simply not able to keep up with the technical progress in all aspects of the game. As a result, her team suffered in league performance.

The third and final reason why division of labor works involves time limitations and the aspect of coaching efficiency. This means that a coach's skill at successfully performing a task increases through repetition. If Dora had allowed Jim to assume the role of assistant coach in charge of post players, both coaches could have focused their efforts exclusively on their respective assignments. Because practice and repetition have been found to improve performance, both Dora and Jim could have improved their coaching effectiveness simply by doing the same thing more often.

In summary, formalizing a division of labor leads to increased coaching effectiveness. Once this division of labor is established, the coach must then learn to delegate responsibility accordingly. Countless textbooks on business administration state that one of the most difficult activities for young administrators is accepting and performing the process of delegation adequately. This applies to coaches as well.

When delegating for success, Kozoll (1985) suggests that you ask yourself the following questions:

- Is this something only you can do?
- If not, to whom can the work be appropriately assigned?
- Is this person prepared now, or does he or she need instruction?

By answering these questions and implementing the answers, you will be well on your way to delegating responsibility successfully. This in turn will improve your coaching effectiveness. If Dora had delegated responsibility for the posts to Jim, the team would have undoubtedly benefited.

Maintain a Well-Defined Authority Hierarchy

The Bible states, "No servant can be the slave of two masters; for either he will hate the first and love the second, or he will be devoted to the first and think nothing of the second" (Matthew 6:24). Most researchers in the area of administration accept the truth in this statement. Maintaining a unity of command is very important in any type of organizational structure. This is especially true in coaching. Think back to the problems encountered by Floundering Frank.

Because the athletic director had encouraged Betty, the assistant coach, to play a major role in team selection and practice sessions, confusion developed regarding Frank's and Betty's responsibilities. The athletes in turn were left wondering who was the real leader on the coaching staff. This whole problem could have been avoided if everyone involved had followed a well-defined authority hierarchy. In this particular example, the athletic director should have established the unity of command necessary for smooth functioning within the team.

If a sport organization is of sufficient size to require multiple coaches, there should be a well-defined hierarchy of positions including the athletic director, the head coach, and the assistant coach. Each lower position is under the supervision and control of a formalized higher position. This facilitates effective supervision and feedback within the sporting environment. It also explicitly defines who has the final say in formal decision-making matters. A similar well-defined distinction between the assistant coach, the team captain, and the other players must also be made explicit. By establishing this chain of command, the potential for unproductive and unpleasant confrontations will be largely eliminated.

Although this organization technique is valuable, make sure you don't go overboard in enforcing it. Maintaining a well-defined authority hierarchy is only a means toward an end, not an end in itself. Always remember that there is no substitute for good communication among team members.

Design Formal Guides to Behavior

To ensure uniform decisions and to regulate the behavior of team members, you should develop and enforce formal rules, policies, and procedures. Codes of ethics, team rules, team policies, and a team policy handbook are examples of written materials you can use to formalize the conditions of participation and standards of behavior expected of athletes. A team policy handbook could cover expected conduct on road trips, required attendance at practice, and guidelines for good sportsmanship, among other topics. In fact, you could state adherence to these written guidelines as an objective in the planning process. This objective could then be evaluated in the usual manner (see chapter 2).

In our earlier example, Coach Tina trusted her team members to act responsibly. Though we all like to believe that our athletes' behavior will always reflect maturity and good judgment, the example illustrates how problems of behavior can arise without formalized guidelines.

If you document codes of behavior, two main results will follow. First, each athlete will know exactly what you expect of him or her. Second, formalized guidelines put you in a better position to consistently enforce these important rules and policies. Things would have worked out much better for Tina if she had used this technique. Many conflicts involving rule enforcement can be avoided if you implement the proper decision-making procedures. In chapter 8, you will learn how effective decision making can improve your overall coaching effectiveness.

Base Decisions on Merit, Not Personality

Your coaching decisions should involve neither your athletes' personalities nor your personal preferences about individual members. To ensure the efficient functioning of your sport team, base all your decisions objectively on previously defined criteria of performance (see chapter 2). Decisions based on personalities rather than on performance can destroy an athletic organization.

Earlier in this chapter, we saw how Coach Pete created unnecessary problems by basing a coaching decision on player personalities rather than on performance. Athletes have to know that their coach's decisions are objective. Only in this manner will they be motivated to improve. For this reason, you should use performance and nonperformance goals (chapter 2) when making decisions like the one made by Personal Pete. If Pete had followed this guideline, his decision might have been the same, but at least he could have justified it with evidence based on the goals for each athlete.

By structuring your sport organization along these four dimensions, you increase the probability of a smoothly running team effort, relatively free of unwanted conflict. This allows you to direct your valuable time and energy toward achieving your primary coaching goals.

SUMMARY AND RECOMMENDATONS

We began by looking at four different coaches and some of the problems they encountered during their competitive seasons. This illustrated the types of problems you can encounter if you do not follow certain organizational principles. In using these principles to improve your coaching, keep the following recommendations in mind:

1. Whenever possible, divide your coaching tasks into smaller components, and delegate some of the responsibility to an assistant coach or team manager. This frees more time for you to concentrate on specific areas that need development. It also allows each individual to keep up with the latest technical advances in his or her area of expertise.
2. If your sport organization or team is too small to warrant more than one coach, consider asking a volunteer to help out with some of the duties. You might involve a parent or university physical education major with an interest in your sport.
3. If you are involved in a large sport organization, make sure there is a well-defined authority hierarchy. With such a structure, everyone knows his or her exact responsibility in the overall coaching effort. This also helps avoid conflict with fellow coaches and sport administrators.
4. It is well worth your time to develop codes of ethics, team rules, and team policies. In fact, a team policy handbook that serves as a formal guide to behavior for your athletes is often a wise idea. This way, each athlete knows exactly what is expected of him or her. As a result, you will avoid many needless conflict situations throughout your season.
5. Never make coaching decisions based on the athletes' personalities or your personal preferences toward individual members. Try to base all your decisions on previously defined criteria of performance. This ensures that all players continue to strive for increased performance levels.

Chapter 4
Organizing a Successful Fund-Raising Campaign

Today's enlightened coach and sport administrator will agree that raising money is rapidly becoming a major concern of almost every contemporary sport organization. Budgetary constraints have seriously affected the amount of financial support available from state and local education funding. When this fact is coupled with the ever-increasing costs of goods and services, you are faced with a serious dilemma. Do you merely maintain the status quo of your organization, or do you seek out creative ways to obtain more funding? With the increasing sophistication of most modern-day sports, maintaining your current level of funding would in actuality result in your organization's falling behind. For this reason it is imperative that you familiarize yourself with the intricacies of successful fund-raising.

Fund-raising can be broken down into two main categories: direct solicitation and indirect solicitation. *Direct solicitation* involves asking potential donors for money to support a particular cause. Little, if anything, is offered donors in return, except for the satisfaction of being associated with a worthy project. With *indirect solicitation* (also known as special events fund-raising), something is given in return for the donated money, such as food, entertainment, merchandise, or services. Although some large sport organizations and teams with well-established public relations programs (e.g., the U.S. Olympic team) can benefit from direct solicitation fund-raising campaigns, this technique is beyond the scope of most teams. For this reason, this chapter

focuses exclusively on developing your awareness of how to use indirect solicitation to raise needed monies for your program.

REASONS WHY PEOPLE DONATE MONEY

For you to be successful in fund-raising, you must understand the psychological reasons that motivate the public to contribute to your cause. Research reveals that the most obvious factor positively motivating contributions is enlightened self-interest—the need to get something out of giving (e.g., the good feeling associated with being able to help someone in need). Other reasons people mention for contributing to fund-raising drives are public acceptance, the need to belong to a worthwhile group or cause, altruism, the desire to help an organization perform work beneficial to others, the gratitude and respect paid to the donor, and the need to outgive members of the donating public.

We could add another very important qualifying point to this list. In a nutshell, most people want to be "sought." Psychologically, they need to feel that their involvement is valued and that they will make a significant contribution. The major implication here is that you must *ask* people to serve your cause. Don't wait for them to volunteer their services.

Regardless of individual reasons for giving, research has indicated that people will, under favorable conditions, donate money to a worthwhile cause. The remainder of this chapter provides you with the information you need to utilize indirect solicitation fund-raising as a viable project for your sport organization or team.

PRINCIPLES FOR SUCCESSFUL FUND-RAISING

The principles of fund-raising are simple, few in number, and easy to apply. As an overview, they include having a worthwhile cause, high-quality leadership, dedicated volunteers, and never-ending public relations. Let's briefly examine each of these principles.

The Cause

Fund-raising involves a small number of people asking a large number of people for money. To justify this request, you must be able to present your cause as being worthy. If you are able to convey a worthy cause and a significant need, then people will donate funds. Therefore, your most important initial objective is to present a good cause that is attractive to potential donors.

As a general guideline, the case for support (or the cause) must relate the needs of the organization or team to larger social endeavors and must provide goals that are demonstrably valid. It is also very important to stress the

urgency and uniqueness of your situation. In other words, you have to convince people why your particular sport organization merits financial support.

An example of a worthwhile cause might be a request for funding to send a local high school girls' gymnastics team to a state competition. This stated need relates to a larger social dimension of community pride. Another worthwhile cause would be a request for money to enable 20 underprivileged children to participate in a community soccer league. This cause ties in with the potential donors' feelings of social responsibility. In both cases, you have conveyed a sincere need that ties in with a larger social theme. The results of donorship in either case are observable. Remember to consider all three dimensions in your stated cause.

Leadership

Before potential leaders can be attracted to commit themselves to your fund-raising project, a worthwhile cause must be identified. If the cause has merit, it is much easier to recruit leaders. Although you may possibly attract a proven leader to your sport organization, it will very likely be the coach or local sport administrator who assumes this role. If not, a committee should be formed to select a suitable candidate. In either case, this individual must display the characteristics of a leader.

Most experts agree that the success of the fund-raising campaign depends on the leader's ability to

- demonstrate enthusiasm,
- attract the interest and loyalty of effective and devoted volunteers,
- spend the required amount of talent and time,
- know how to use the committee system (conducting meetings, delegating responsibilities, etc.), and
- never doubt victory.

Some sport organizations may be fortunate enough to appoint a well-respected community leader or local sport hero in the position of chairperson or co-chairperson. This individual may or may not be involved in doing the actual work but certainly has the potential to inspire others to do it. That is why many universities select former successful athletes as athletic directors. From a psychological standpoint, people derive a sense of pride by associating with known leaders. This in turn may increase a potential donor's desire to contribute to your cause. The ability to raise funds is directly proportional to the caliber and commitment of the organization's leader.

Volunteers

The success or failure of your fund-raising campaign is also determined in a large measure by the dedication, energy, and enthusiasm of the volunteers. These are the individuals who help plan and organize the process as well as perform much of the work.

Research indicates that volunteer motivation is best maintained if the leader incorporates the element of fun into the entire process. Obviously, as a leader you will develop greater worker satisfaction if volunteers enjoy participating in every stage of planning and organizing. Don't hold a long, boring indoctrination meeting; make it into a pleasant social event. During this initial get-together, solicit and discuss the volunteers' ideas. Participatory management theory suggests that volunteers who have shared in the decision-making process are more committed to a successful outcome.

When you are delegating responsibilities, you can ensure greater worker satisfaction by allowing volunteers to choose the tasks that best align with their particular interests and talents. For example, some individuals may not feel comfortable asking people for money but may enjoy record-keeping duties. By actively seeking out individual preferences, the fund-raising process will be built on the volunteers' strengths rather than their weaknesses.

Volunteers are normally recruited from within the sport organization—for example, coaches, trainers, assistant coaches, and the athletes themselves. This usually nets good results because the volunteers are already committed to the cause. By recruiting volunteers from within your organization, you also ensure an element of continuity within your fund-raising program. This is very important if fund-raising is going to be an annual event or an ongoing process.

One last concern in this area is the issue of using professional fund-raisers rather than volunteers. In planning a fund-raising drive, your sport organization may have the option of hiring professionals instead of developing the necessary manpower from within the organization. Although professional fund-raisers do exist, I do not normally recommend that either educational institutions or sport organizations employ them. These individuals not only cost a lot of money, but often their involvement in your organization results in bad public relations. It makes more sense from a community standpoint to keep all the money raised within the organization or team.

Public Relations

Public relations is vital to a successful fund-raising campaign. Without the positive climate created by an ongoing public relations program, fund-raising will fail or be severely limited. Public philanthropy is based on the public's awareness of your sport program. This necessitates that sport organizations conduct their public relations programs on a year-round basis.

Ignoring the importance of public relations until the eve of a fund-raising campaign almost always results in total failure. Keeping this in mind, here are a few suggestions on how you can keep your team in the public eye:

- Attempt to maintain an annual schedule that includes alumni games and friendly competitions between athletes and parents (when applicable).
- Take frequent advantage of opportunities to display your organization in action, such as during a gymnastics night, a high school athletic open house, or sports clinics.
- Keep the media informed of all upcoming competitions as well as results. Remember to use all media forms. These services are usually free for your asking. Holding a media day with your team may win you the goodwill of the local television, radio, and newspaper sport directors.
- Consider designing team buttons, jackets, bumper stickers, or some other form of highly visible identification. This provides

your team or athletic organization with a year-round public relations campaign.

The previous examples are by no means an exhaustive list. The number of ways you can keep your team or sport organization in the public eye is limited only by your effort and ingenuity. It is important to remember, however, that the best foundation for successful public relations is a sound program. The most elaborate public relations program can never make up for basic defects in a poorly run organization. Running a smooth, well-organized program will gain you excellent word-of-mouth public relations.

INDIRECT SOLICITATION FUND-RAISING

For the average team or sport organization, special events fund-raising offers several distinct advantages. It can

- provide financial gain;
- increase public awareness;
- improve public relations;
- make direct, door-to-door solicitation unnecessary;
- require less manpower than direct solicitation; and
- be versatile.

Special events may be large or small, elaborate or simple, and directed to any interest group. For these reasons, it is important for you to become familiar with the intricacies of special events fund-raising. Let's take a closer look at the actual mechanics of using indirect solicitation techniques.

We have already discussed the importance of four underlying principles of successful fund-raising: developing a worthwhile cause, choosing the right leader, recruiting good volunteers, and establishing an ongoing public relations program. You can develop your actual special events fund-raising plan only after these principles have been satisfied. When this has been done, you are ready to proceed with the following specific stages:

- Determining a suitable event
- Implementing and organizing the event
- Wrapping up and evaluating the project

Determining a Suitable Event

Generally speaking, there are nine types of fund-raising projects. Though only a few examples are given here for each category, the number of possible events is limited only by your imagination.

- Selling something that people want to buy—such as light bulbs or chocolates
- Social activities—dances, hayrides
- Putting on the feed bag—a pancake breakfast, doughnut days
- Social settings—auctions, arts and crafts
- Games of chance—bingo, raffles, lotteries, casino nights
- Entertainment—celebrity show, local variety
- Sporting events—horse show, celebrity tournament
- Providing services—car wash, grass cutting
- Sponsorship—skate-a-thon, basket-a-thon

When selecting the event you want to hold, keep this in mind: Safe events are those that involve little capital outlay. Providing services, therefore, is one of the safest events, because all you need is a group of willing volunteers. Hosting a car wash or providing grass-cutting services involves little, if any, initial outlay of money. Volunteers can use their own buckets, sponges, and lawn mowers. You just can't lose money! Selling something that people want to buy is also safe, provided that unsold merchandise can be returned.

On the other hand, staging events that involve a larger capital outlay (such as a dance featuring a popular and therefore expensive band) is riskier, because attendance is an unknown factor. Your organization could actually lose money after paying the band if attendance is poor. If your event has been properly planned, however, the team or sport organization will usually reap a respectable profit from any of the nine fund-raising categories.

As a general guideline, the profitability of the event you sponsor depends greatly on your selecting the right event. Before you make a decision, you need well-researched, honest, and realistic answers to some very important questions.

What Is the Team's or Organization's Goal?

Before you can decide on a suitable fund-raising event, you must first determine your organization's financial goal. In calculating how much money you need, consider two main factors: Why you need the money and how much it will cost to sponsor the event.

A detailed plan on how the money is going to be spent usually attracts more sponsors; therefore, be sure to include in your publicity campaign the reason you are trying to raise money. The second consideration, how much it will cost you to raise the money you need, requires that you prepare a detailed budget. Only in this manner can you accurately assess the costs and benefits of the fund-raising event to your sport organization. A sample detailed budget or financial plan for a specific fund-raiser is provided below.

From the financial plan, you can see that this particular team or sport organization has the potential to raise $1,035 after all expenses have been covered. It is important to note, however, that this projection assumes that all

---

Projected Budget—Teen Rock Dance
(Sample)

Estimated expenditures

1. *Salaries*

Secretary	2 hr @ $7.50/hr	$ 15	
Janitor	3 hr @ $15/hr	$ 45	
Band	Flat fee	$ 200	
Chaperones	(Volunteers, no charge)	$ 0	
	Subtotal		$ 260

2. *Office*

Telephone	Correspondence with band	$ 25	
Xerox	300 flyers @ 15¢/copy	$ 45	
Auditorium	Donated by high school	$ 0	
	Subtotal		$ 70

3. *Refreshments*

Pop	12 cases (288 cans) @ $7/case	$ 84	
Milk	50 cartons @ 30¢/carton	$ 15	
Chips/pretzels	200 bags @ 20¢/bag	$ 40	
Doughnuts	10 dozen @ $2.50/dozen	$ 25	
	Subtotal		$ 164
	Projected expenses		$ 494

Estimated income

1. *Dance*

Tickets	250 @ $5/each	$1,250	
	Subtotal		$1,250

2. *Refreshments*

Pop	288 cans @ 50¢/can	$ 144	
Milk	50 cartons @ 50¢/carton	$ 25	
Chips/pretzels	200 bags @ 40¢/bag	$ 80	
Doughnuts	120 @ 25¢/each	$ 30	
	Subtotal		$ 279
	Projected income		$1,529

tickets and refreshments will be sold. If this does not happen, the net funds raised will be reduced accordingly.

What Are Your Financial and Human Resources?

It does take money to make money—this idea certainly holds true for fund-raising. If you have a large financial goal, you will probably have to invest a substantial amount of money up front. For example, you could hire a top-name entertainer for your fund-raising project, which would increase the event's drawing power and thereby result in larger revenues, but it would also require a larger capital outlay. This in turn poses a greater financial risk to your organization. It is always advisable to err on the conservative side when planning a fund-raising event. Your choice of a fund-raising event, then, is largely determined by your organization's budget. Proceed with a high-cost event only if you are reasonably sure that it will be successful.

Another limiting factor to consider is your human resources. The one absolutely essential ingredient of a successful fund-raiser is people—dedicated, hard-working, self-sacrificing, and cooperative individuals. In selecting your event, make sure that it corresponds to the interests, talents, and capacity of your volunteer human resources.

Finally, when determining your volunteer resources, think about individuals not directly associated with your sport organization. Friends and families of team members, as well as community leaders, are examples of individuals who have much to offer your event.

Who Is Your Target Market?

The whole idea of special event fund-raising is to offer potential customers something they want. If you have conducted successful events in the past, you will have a wealth of valuable information regarding your target market. You will be familiar with the type of activity that is most popular in your community. Remember, what works in one city or neighborhood might not necessarily work in another.

Communities vary in terms of interests, ethnic backgrounds, geographical considerations, and other things. Don't make the mistake of attempting to copy a successful fund-raising event that was conducted elsewhere. Even though you can learn from those events and get valuable ideas, it is important to remember that communities vary greatly in terms of what they want for entertainment or services. For example, in some communities soccer is the most popular sport. In others, it might be baseball or football. In planning a sporting event fund-raiser, this information is vitally important to your ultimate financial success. Always try to tailor your fund-raising event to the interests of the community in which the event will be staged. Doing your homework to define your target market is the best approach and will prove to be time well spent.

What Timing Is Best for Your Event?

Determining when and how often the special event fund-raising project should be staged is a critical issue. First and foremost, timing is determined by when you need the money for your team or sport organization. If you are traveling to a state championship, for example, you will need the money well in advance of your competition date.

The decision about when to hold the event is also determined largely by the amount of lead time necessary to plan and develop the project. Smaller projects (e.g., a car wash) might require only a few weeks, whereas larger events (e.g., a dinner and dance) might require several months or even a year to develop.

Determining the proper "when" also involves seasonal considerations. For example, the best time to conduct a special events fund-raising project for a hockey team is when community interest is at a peak. One appropriate time might be immediately preceding the season, because people are gearing up for the sport. During your league's playoffs, or the period immediately following them, is another good opportunity. The Stanley Cup playoffs could also be an excellent time. Make sure you consider the "when" factor if you want your project to raise optimal funds.

The second timing consideration that you must address involves how often to hold the event. It could be annual, semiannual, or even ongoing (such as a concession booth). Some extremely large projects are held only every 2 or 3 years because of their magnitude. In making your decision on how often to hold an event, consider the demands it places on your human resources and how often people are willing to pay money to support your cause.

Finally, to ensure the success of your special event, make sure that it doesn't conflict with another similar project in the community. This could seriously affect your revenues.

Implementing and Organizing

By this time you have developed a worthwhile cause, established a financial goal, and selected an event. Your attention must now be focused on the actual organization of the fund-raising program. Most of the time the leader performs the actual organization. Once again, this points out the need to have a very competent individual in this role. As a coach or sport administrator, you will probably assume this position.

One of the leader's first organizational tasks is to establish the appropriate committees. If your event is relatively small, you may need only one committee. With larger projects, it is wise to delegate responsibility as discussed in chapter 3. Form small, manageable committees that are each responsible for one specific function.

For example, a program development committee should be formed to undertake all aspects of program planning. This group is responsible for determining the different functions required to make your fund-raiser a success. Let's say this committee determines that the areas of publicity, volunteer recruitment, and evaluation and wrap-up require special attention. As leader, you would then form additional committees to address each of these issues. A publicity committee would be responsible for all aspects of public relations, promotion, and advertising. The sole responsibility of this group would be to keep your team or sport organization in the public eye by maintaining publicity throughout the duration of the fund-raiser. The volunteer recruitment committee would determine and then seek out the volunteers needed to make your project successful. The evaluation and wrap-up committee would be responsible for the complete analysis of your fund-raiser in terms of what went right and what didn't. It would also be responsible for all wrap-up procedures, including preparing a financial statement, sending letters of thanks to contributors, drawing up a list of suggestions for future fund-raisers, and organizing a "thank-you" party for your volunteers.

It is a good idea at this stage of the fund-raising project to get your workers together to brainstorm about all of the things that could possibly go wrong with your event. Anticipating potential problems enables you to develop plans and contingency plans to avoid the pitfalls.

The actual implementation of the fund-raising project involves developing an organizational structure that stresses division of labor. This not only makes the most efficient use of your human resources; it also makes the overall task much more manageable. In planning and implementing your fund-raising event, consider using an organizational worksheet to help you focus your early efforts. A sample worksheet is included on pages 32 and 33. Feel free to copy it for your use.

In the initial stages, it is best to identify a variety of options for each question. As you progress in your planning and consultation efforts, the best alternatives will begin to surface. Remember, this worksheet is intended only as an organization tool to focus your early efforts. It is not intended as a substitute for valuable committee input.

Wrapping Up and Evaluating

In concluding your fund-raising project, I recommend several specific wrap-up procedures. First, you should prepare a financial report. This is done by substituting actual expenditures and revenues for the ones projected in the budget (see p. 29). This financial statement then serves as a springboard for discussing and evaluating your fund-raising event. Second, if you plan to engage in future fund-raising events, the best time to begin preparations is immediately. For this reason, hold a meeting to discuss any areas that could have been improved. Allow only constructive criticism at this meeting.

The third step in the wrap-up procedure involves evaluating your organizational structure. Analyze the number of committees and the number of workers assigned to individual tasks to determine if more efficient organization was possible.

Fund-Raising Organization Worksheet

1. What are some worthwhile causes that our team or sport organization can claim?

2. Who can we approach to be project leader (if other than the coach or sport administrator)?

3. What are some potential sources of volunteers?

4. How much money does our team or organization need?

5. What are some possible target markets that we can approach?

6. What special events would best serve the target markets identified in item 5?

7. How much money will we have to spend to raise these funds? (Specify possible expenses.)

8. Once raised, how will the funds be utilized?

9. When would be the best times to stage our fund-raiser?

10. What evaluation wrap-up procedures should we follow after the fund-raiser is over?

Another very important wrap-up task is drawing up a complete list of all those individuals outside your sport organization who donated money, merchandise, or services to your project. Send thank-you notes to these individuals outlining your financial results and each donor's part in the fund-raiser's success. Finally, consider having a wrap-up party for all your workers. After all, these individuals were largely responsible for the success of your fund-raising event.

In conducting your wrap-up and evaluation procedures, consider using a form similar to the one on page 35 to record the strengths and weaknesses of your fund-raising event.

SUMMARY AND RECOMMENDATIONS

When you decide to embark on an indirect fund-raising venture, you may wish to use the checklist on page 36 as a summary review and organization tool. Once each phase of the fund-raiser is finalized, place a check mark (✔) beside that item. By working through the checklist, you will be following the most logical sequence of development.

As you consider the possibility of raising needed money for your sport organization, keep the following recommendations in mind:

1. Take a close look at your team's or sport organization's budget. If financial resources are curbing the effectiveness of your program, the time is right to consider fund-raising as a viable alternative.

2. Indirect solicitation (also known as special events fund-raising) is recommended for most sport organizations. This method puts less strain on your human and financial resources.

3. The role of the leader in organizing a successful fund-raising event cannot be overstated. As coach or sport administrator, you will likely assume this important position. Remember, it is your enthusiasm and attention to detail that will determine if the project turns out to be a success or a failure. Chapter 6 is designed to improve your leadership effectiveness.

4. Make sure you pay special attention to the five Ws of indirect fund-raising:

   - What is your sport organization's goal?
   - What are your financial and human resources?
   - Who is your target market?
   - What event is best for this target market?
   - What timing is best for the event?

Sample Evaluation Form

Looking back at our fund-raising event, what features turned out to be our major strengths?

What features turned out to be our major weaknesses?

What could improve our future fund-raising efforts?

Other thoughts, observations, or comments on our fund-raiser?

Checklist for Indirect Solicitation Fund-Raising

_____ A worthwhile cause has been developed.

_____ The project leader has been established.

_____ Prospective volunteers have been identified.

_____ Committees and committee chairpersons have been identified (when appropriate).

_____ Initial publicity plans have been formulated.

_____ A financial goal for the fund-raising project has been determined.

_____ A plan for utilization of funds raised has been developed.

_____ Your financial and human resources have been developed.

_____ A projected budget has been drawn up.

_____ Your target market has been established.

_____ A decision has been made regarding the special events to be offered.

_____ The timing of your event has been determined.

_____ Evaluation/wrap-up procedures have been planned.

_____ A plan for acknowledging those individuals who helped make your event a success has been developed.

_____ A meeting has been planned to evaluate the fund-raising event.

_____ A wrap-up party has been planned to thank the workers for their efforts.

Notes:

Chapter 5
Organizing Competition

By now you have come to appreciate just how much your athletes enjoy participating in formal competitions. After all, that's why they're involved in the first place. Though we normally associate tournament competition with the season-end selection of champions, tournament play can also serve a variety of other functions. Successful coaches realize that the tournament structure can also be used effectively in the practice situation. The values of organizing tournament play in practices include the following:

- It stimulates interest and helps develop excellence in the physical activity.
- It provides challenging competition and healthy activity.
- It prepares athletes for higher-level competitions in the future.
- It can be used to select a team.
- It can be used to declare a champion.
- It provides simulated competition, thereby acclimating your players to the stress of competition.

Because of these reasons, it is important to familiarize yourself with the proper techniques of organizing tournament draws. This information will also enable you to host your own tournament if the situation arises. The remainder of this chapter examines the different types of tournaments that are most commonly used in the coaching environment:

- Single elimination
- Consolation
- Double elimination
- Bagnall-Wild
- Round-robin
- Challenge formats (ladder)

If you would like to learn more about these or other tournament structures, consult *Organizing Successful Tournaments* (Byl, 1990).

SINGLE ELIMINATION

One of the most common forms of athletic competition is the traditional single elimination tournament. Many coaches feel that this type of tournament is the least desirable because it emphasizes the elimination of teams and players. For example, in this type of tournament, half the competitors are eliminated after their first contest. However, this format of competition is still valuable in certain circumstances.

When to Use This Type of Tournament

You would probably choose the single elimination format if you have limited time and facilities to run your competition (e.g., a weekend tennis tournament), or if you have many participants (e.g., 120 entries in the men's "C" racquetball division). In many instances, a single elimination tournament may be the only way you can accommodate all of the players. An additional reason for choosing this technique concerns the nature of activity you are coaching. For example, if the activity is sufficiently strenuous and intense (such as boxing, wrestling, or sprinting), a large number of matches is impractical. In activities such as these, you would be wise to choose the single elimination format. Finally, if you are concerned only with determining one winner, the single elimination tournament is an acceptable format.

Procedure for Setting Up the Draw

The first step in arranging a single elimination tournament is to determine whether the number of entries is an even power of 2 (i.e., 2, 4, 8, 16, 32, 64, etc.). If so, then proceed by drawing for position. For example, suppose you want to arrange a competition for eight teams. Because 8 is an even power of 2, you can set up the tournament as shown in Figure 5.1.

As you can see from Figure 5.1, Team B was drawn for the first position, Team D for the second, and so on. This procedure can be accomplished by either picking names or teams out of a hat, or having the athletes draw numbers for positions.

When the number of entrants is not an even power of 2, you must arrange byes. Assigning these "free matches" allows you to avoid having an uneven number of teams or players left to compete in the semifinal or final rounds. All byes must be placed in the first round. This ensures that the number of contestants for the second round is an even power of 2. You can accomplish this by subtracting the total number of entrants from the next higher power of 2. For example, if you have 13 entrants, subtract 13 from the next higher power of 2, which in this case is 16. This leaves 3, which is the number of byes you need. The total number of entrants (13) minus the 3 byes leaves 10 contestants to play each other in the first round (see Figure 5.2). Five will lose,

leaving 8 contestants in the second round. Because 8 is an even power of 2, 4 teams will reach the semifinals, and only 2 can now meet in the final round.

Most coaches are familiar with the concept of seeding. This refers to the process of placing superior competitors (based on their past performance and reputation) in separate brackets or as far away from each other as possible in the same bracket. This minimizes the chances that these individuals will meet in the early rounds, thereby eliminating one of them. If you have two seeded players, place one at the top of the upper bracket and the other at the bottom of the lower bracket. If two more entrants are seeded, place the third at the top of the lower bracket and the fourth seed at the bottom of the upper bracket as illustrated in Figure 5.3 (see page 40).

If there are byes, seeded players should get them in order of their ranking (see Figure 5.3). Thus, give the number-one seed the first bye, number two the second bye, and so on. Remember, no player or team ever receives more than one bye, and seeding should be employed only when the teams' previous records justify it.

One last hint in setting up single elimination tournaments involves calculating the number of games required to complete the tournament. Remember that the number of games in a single elimination tournament is always one less than the number of entries. For example, with 13 entries, 12 games are required to complete the tournament.

The advantages and disadvantages of using a single elimination tournament are listed in

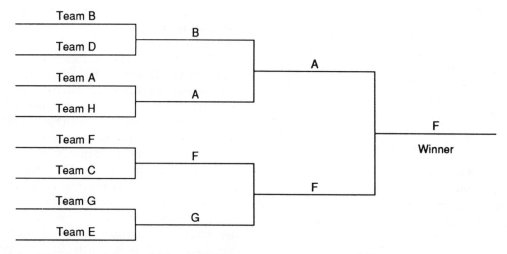

Figure 5.1. The bracket for a single elimination tournament with eight teams.

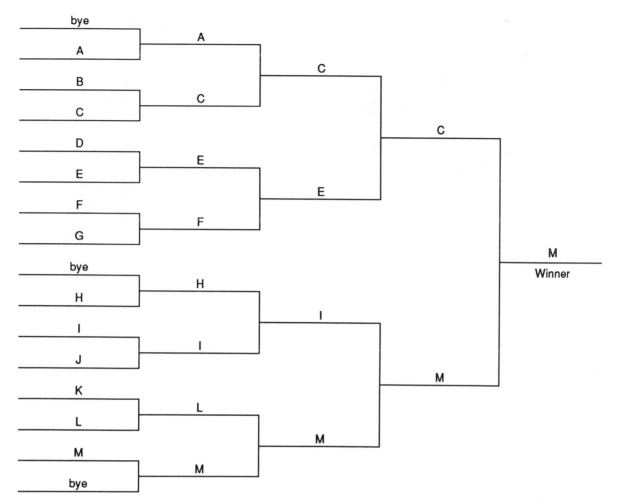

Figure 5.2. The bracket for a single elimination tournament with 13 teams.

Table 5.1. Consider these pros and cons carefully before deciding to use this tournament format.

Table 5.1
Advantages and Disadvantages
of the Single Elimination Tournament

Advantages	Disadvantages
The tournament takes a short time; a winner is selected quickly.	It emphasizes elimination.
It is good for limited facilities.	The eventual winner is not always the best entrant.
It is good for a large number of entries.	The defeated finalist is not always second-best.
The tournament is exciting for both players and spectators.	

CONSOLATION ELIMINATION TOURNAMENT

Many people think this type of tournament is superior to the single elimination format because it permits each player or team to play at least twice. This way, a very good player or team eliminated in the first round can continue to play with the chance of winning secondary honors. Because more games are involved, this form of competition usually produces greater player enthusiasm than the single elimination format.

When to Use This Type of Tournament

Consolation tournaments are recommended in circumstances where adequate time and facilities are available to accommodate the extra number of games. Also, when teams or players

Figure 5.3. The bracket for a single elimination tournament for 13 teams with 4 seeded entries.

have to travel long distances to the competition site, it is a good idea to use a consolation format because each participant is guaranteed at least two contests, making the journey much more worthwhile. Finally, even if you have a fairly large number of entries, a consolation tournament can still be run fairly quickly in comparison to the other competition formats that are examined later in this chapter.

Procedure for Setting Up the Draw

There are two general types of consolation elimination tournaments. One type, which is seldom used, provides the opportunity for any loser to win the consolation round regardless of when the initial loss occurs. For example, a defeated finalist is given the opportunity to play in the consolation final. Because this

method is rarely used, we will focus our attention on the traditional consolation approach. The procedure for this format is simply that all the losers in the first round (as well as those who lose in the second round after receiving a first-round bye) play another single elimination tournament. The person or team that wins this second tournament is deemed the consolation winner. Figure 5.4 illustrates how this competition would be arranged if there were no byes. Figure 5.5 illustrates how the tournament would be arranged if byes were necessary.

In Figure 5.5 you will notice that entry A enters the consolation round after losing in the second round to entry C. This is because A received a bye in the first round. This same procedure would have been followed if entry F had lost to entry D. The easiest way to remember this is to place all losers of their first game in the consolation bracket, which is

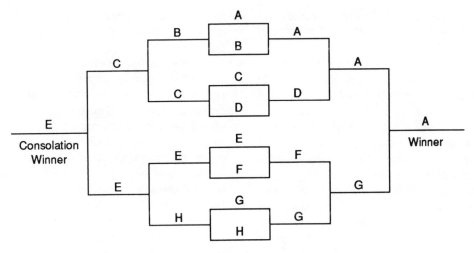

Figure 5.4.   The brackets for a consolation tournament for eight entries.

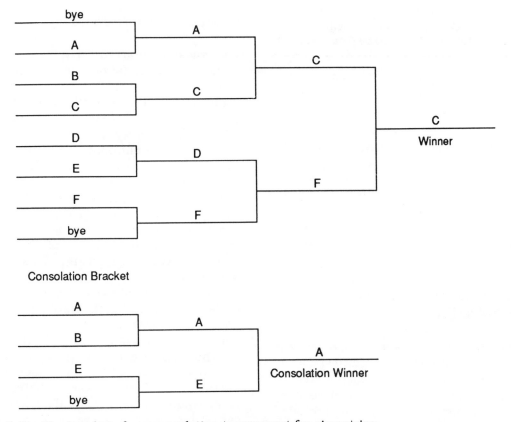

Figure 5.5.   The brackets for a consolation tournament for six entries.

set up as any other single elimination tournament.

To calculate the number of games required to complete this tournament format, remember that the consolation elimination tournament is really a single elimination tournament that moves to the right with an added conso-

lation tournament that moves to the left (see Figure 5.4). The tournament moving to the right requires one less game than the number of entries, in this case 7 games (8 − 1). Once this first round is played, 4 entries remain to play the consolation round moving to the left. This requires an additional 3 games (4 − 1).

A total of 10 games (7 + 3) are therefore required to complete a consolation elimination tournament with 8 entries.

Using this same technique, the tournament outlined in Figure 5.5 requires 5 games (6 − 1) to complete the winner's bracket and 2 games (3 − 1) to complete the consolation bracket. In total, then, 7 games are required to complete a consolation tournament with 6 entries. This calculation technique will work regardless of the number of entries.

The advantages and disadvantages of the consolation elimination format are summarized in Table 5.2. Use these pros and cons to determine if this format is best for your purposes.

**Table 5.2
Advantages and Disadvantages
of the Consolation Elimination Tournament**

Advantages	Disadvantages
Each entry plays at least twice.	It is more time-consuming to run.
A good entry eliminated by the champion early in the tournament may continue.	More games are involved, causing a potential space problem when there is a large number of entries.
Greater player interest is maintained.	

DOUBLE ELIMINATION TOURNAMENT

With this tournament format, each entry is assured of playing at least two contests. However, after losing twice, a contestant is eliminated. This format is a variation of the consolation format; losers of any match are included in the consolation bracket. The final match of the tournament is between the winner of the winner's bracket and the winner of the loser's bracket.

When to Use This Type of Tournament

If you have a lot of time available or fewer entries than was the case with the preceding two formats, consider using the double elimination tournament. This format results in the selection of a more adequate winner because it allows for the possibility of a strong entry having one bad game or match but still having the potential to win the championship. Because a team or athlete must lose twice to be eliminated from championship play, it results in greater player motivation throughout the entire tournament. Double elimination tournaments have become quite popular in softball, tennis, wrestling, and other sports. The main point to remember is that you will need more time to run this draw than is necessary with the single elimination or consolation elimination formats.

Procedure for Setting Up the Draw

The brackets are arranged in the same way as in the single elimination tournament. Seeding is also performed in the same manner. The contestants that lose in the first round move to the left, and the winners advance to the right. Subsequently, when a team on the left loses again, it is eliminated because it has two losses. When a team on the right loses, it moves over to the loser's side (the left). If that participant loses again, he or she is eliminated. Because a contestant is not eliminated until he or she loses twice, the winner of the loser's bracket meets the winner of the winner's bracket for the championship. This procedure is illustrated in Figure 5.6.

In double elimination tournaments, the formula for determining the number of games is $2N − 1$ or 2, where N is the number of entries. For example, in Figure 5.6 we have 4 entries. The number of games required to complete this tournament is $(2 \times 4) − 1$ or 2, which means either 7 or 6 games. The number of games required can vary for the following reason. Refer back to Figure 5.6—if contestant D wins the championship match against A, then at that point both A and D have lost only one match each. Because this is a double elimination tournament, A and D have to play each other a second time so that only one competitor remains who has not lost two matches. This calculation technique will work regardless of the number of entries.

The advantages and disadvantages of the double elimination tournament are summa-

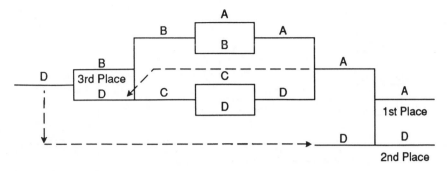

Figure 5.6. The brackets for a double elimination tournament for four entries.

Table 5.3
Advantages and Disadvantages
of the Double Elimination Tournament

Advantages	Disadvantages
A player or team must be beaten twice to be eliminated.	It takes longer to run.
	It emphasizes elimination.
It selects a more adequate winner.	
It maintains player motivation right up until the end.	

rized in Table 5.3. Consider these points in determining if the double elimination format is best for your purposes.

BAGNALL-WILD ELIMINATION TOURNAMENT

This is actually a modified form of the single elimination and consolation elimination tournaments. It was designed for the purpose of selecting true second- and third-place winners.

When to Use This Type of Tournament

As mentioned above, you should consider using the Bagnall-Wild format whenever you are especially interested in second- and third-place finishes. For example, if you want to organize a competition to select a three-person team, this form of competition gives you the best results. It is also useful when a point system is in operation, with points awarded for each of the top three finishers.

Procedure for Setting Up the Draw

The first step in this procedure involves determining first place by means of single elimination play. To determine second place, take all competitors who have lost to the champion before the final round and have them compete against each other in a mini-elimination tournament. The winner of this mini-tournament then plays the defeated finalist for second place. You can then determine third place by having all entries defeated by the second-place finisher compete in another mini-tournament. This whole process is illustrated in Figure 5.7.

To calculate the number of games required, remember that a Bagnall-Wild format starts out as a single elimination tournament. The number of games required to determine first place, then, is one less than the total number of entries. In our example in Figure 5.7 with 8 entries, 7 games ($N - 1$) are required to determine first place. To calculate the number of games required to determine second place, count the number of opponents defeated by the champion E (3 in this case—F, H, and A), then subtract one from that number ($N - 1$ again). Follow this procedure for calculating the number of games required to determine third place. Because three opponents (B, C, and F) were defeated by the second-place finisher A, then 2 games ($3 - 1$) are required to determine third place. Therefore, a total of 11 games ($7 + 2 + 2$) are required to complete a Bagnall-Wild tournament with 8 entries. This same formula can be used regardless of the number of entrants.

It is important to note, however, that if the

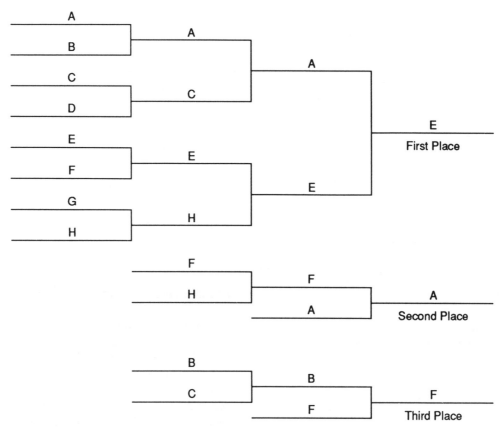

Figure 5.7.   The brackets for a Bagnall-Wild tournament for eight entries.

defeated finalist (Entry A) loses the match for second place against Entry F, then F becomes the second-place winner, leaving Entry A the third-place winner, because A has already defeated B and C.

The playoffs for second and third place should begin as soon as the two finalists (Entries A and E in this case) have been established. Therefore, before the finals take place, Entries B and C and Entries F and H should play their matches. This reduces the amount of play necessary after the winning finalist has been determined. Advantages and disadvantages of this format are listed in Table 5.4.

ROUND-ROBIN TOURNAMENTS

In the round-robin tournament, each player or team gets to play every other player or team at least once. In a single round-robin, each entry plays every other entry once. In a double round-robin, each competitor plays two games with every other entry.

When to Use This Type of Tournament

The round-robin tournament is the best competition format to use if sufficient time and facilities are available or if the number of entries is small. Most coaches are familiar with round-robin play. If you want to determine a true winner and at the same time rank the other contestants in the best possible manner, the round-robin tournament is your best alternative. For example, to select a varsity badminton or table tennis team, simply have the athletes who attend tryouts compete in a round-robin tournament. The results can be one of the tools you use for selecting the team.

Procedures for Setting Up the Draw

If you have an even number of entries, arrange two vertical columns of numbers representing the number of entries. This is done by listing the numbers consecutively down the first column and up the second. With each number representing a team, this provides the pairings

Table 5.4
Advantages and Disadvantages
of the Bagnall-Wild Elimination Tournament

Advantages	Disadvantages
It selects true second- and third-place winners.	The major weakness involves the necessary delay following the first round before competitors for second and third place can be matched, because the finalists must be determined before the tournament can proceed.
It can accommodate a large number of entries in a relatively short period of time.	
	Second- and third-place winners may be more accurately determined than the overall first-place finisher.

for the first round. To obtain the pairings for the following rounds, rotate all the numbers counterclockwise around one of the numbers that remains fixed (usually the number in the top left position). Continue this procedure until all pairings have been exhausted (i.e., you arrive back at your original pairings of numbers). This whole process is illustrated in Figure 5.8.

Round 1	Round 2	Round 3	Round 4	Round 5
1 vs. 6	1 vs. 5	1 vs. 4	1 vs. 3	1 vs. 2
2 vs. 5	6 vs. 4	5 vs. 3	4 vs. 2	3 vs. 6
3 vs. 4	2 vs. 3	6 vs. 2	5 vs. 6	4 vs. 5

Figure 5.8. The round-robin pairings for six entries.

The process is the same with an uneven number of entries. In this case, however, a bye should be placed in one of the positions (again, usually the top left), and the other numbers are rotated around it as illustrated in Figure 5.9.

After each competitor has played every other competitor, the ranking of the entrants is determined by percentages. To do this, divide each participant's number of games won by the total number of games played. In this

Round 1	Round 2	Round 3	Round 4	Round 5
bye - 5	bye - 4	bye - 3	bye - 2	bye - 1
1 vs. 4	5 vs. 3	4 vs. 2	3 vs. 1	2 vs. 5
2 vs. 3	1 vs. 2	5 vs. 1	4 vs. 5	3 vs. 4

Figure 5.9. The round-robin pairings for five entries.

calculation a tie counts as one half of a win. For example, if a player wins five games, loses two, and ties one, the percentage is .688 (5.5 ÷ 8). Participants are then ranked by their percentage points.

The formula for determining the total number of games to be played in a round-robin tournament is $[N(N-1)]/2$, with N representing the number of teams or participating units in the tournament. Using our example in Figure 5.8, a round-robin tournament with 6 entries requires $6(6-1)/2$, or 15 games. This formula can be used with any number of entries.

Advantages and disadvantages of the round-robin format are included in Table 5.5. Consider them carefully before choosing this format.

Table 5.5
Advantages and Disadvantages
of the Round-Robin Tournament

Advantages	Disadvantages
It selects a true winner; it is more representative.	It takes a longer time to complete.
It ranks all competitors.	More facilities are required.
It permits continuous play with maximum use of facilities.	

CHALLENGE TOURNAMENTS

The last type of organized competition that we will look at is one that can be carried on by the players independently or without any formal schedules. Challenge or ladder tournaments are most often used for singles or doubles competition rather than for team sports.

When to Use This Type of Tournament

Challenge tournaments are most commonly used for activities such as tennis, badminton, squash, racquetball, table tennis, handball, wrestling, and archery. This type of competition can be of special value to you as a coach when you need to select team members in individual sports. Many wrestling coaches use the ladder tournament to select the competitors in each weight class from one week to the next.

Although there are many varieties of challenge tournaments, we will focus our attention exclusively on the traditional ladder tournament because of its expediency and simplicity for selecting team members.

Procedure for Setting Up the Draw

First, contestants' names are placed on cards that can be either placed in slots or hung on hooks. Once you have all the names on the cards, initiate the tournament by drawing the cards out of a hat and placing them in the order drawn from the top of the ladder down to the last rung. Seeding is not involved in challenge tournaments. At this point, your typical ladder tournament looks something like the one illustrated in Figure 5.10.

Once the ladder has been set up as illustrated, the following rules govern play:

- A standard criterion defines a win (e.g., best two of three games, one game, and so on).
- Players may advance by challenging and defeating a competitor, or by default if the challenge is not accepted.
- A player may challenge only up to two players above him- or herself (e.g., in Figure 5.10 Julie could challenge only Linda or Sue).
- If a challenger wins, he or she trades card positions with the defeated contestant.
- Challenges must be played in the order they are made.
- After two contestants have played, they cannot play each other again until each has played another contestant at least once.
- A defender must play within 3 days (or whatever the coach or sport administrator deems appropriate) or default.

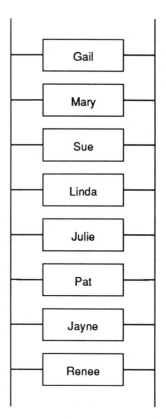

Figure 5.10. The ladder challenge tournament.

- The player at the top of the ladder at the end of a specified time period (e.g., 2 weeks, 10 days, 3 months, etc.) is the winner.

The advantages and disadvantages of the ladder tournament are listed in Table 5.6. Con-

Table 5.6
Advantages and Disadvantages of the Ladder Challenge Tournament

Advantages	Disadvantages
The activity can be carried on independently by the athletes without the presence of the coach or sport administrator.	Over a period of time, players often end up competing with the same people.
It affords competition with contestants of near equal ability.	Over a period of time, it can become less exciting.
No one is eliminated, thus play is continuous for all contestants.	The coach does not have the same degree of contact with the athletes as in the other formats.

sider them carefully before deciding on the ladder format.

SUMMARY AND RECOMMENDATIONS

This chapter has presented you with all the information you need to conduct six different types of organized competition. You can employ these techniques in practice to stimulate interest and help develop excellence in your athletes, provide challenging competition within your team, prepare your players for higher levels of competition, and simulate competitive situations that your athletes are likely to encounter. The information is also of special value in running tournaments or organizing play days. Last, but certainly not least, you can utilize one or any combination of these competition formats to choose your team. In closing, I offer the following recommendations:

1. The judicious practice of organized competition can provide your athletes with a competitive edge against their opponents.
2. If you wish to use these techniques to choose your team, consider using the Bagnall-Wild, round-robin, and ladder tournaments. They will provide you with more representative selections.
3. Familiarize yourself with the intricacies of each type of tournament draw. By knowing the proper procedures for each tournament format, you are able to ensure that your athletes are not victimized by an incorrect draw.

Chapter 6
Developing Your Leadership Skills

Successful sport teams usually have one major attribute that sets them apart from unsuccessful teams: dynamic and effective leadership. Although most of us would agree with this idea, there seems to be much less consensus on just what being a dynamic and effective leader entails. As a coach, you have probably already asked yourself the following questions:

- What is leadership?
- What makes an effective leader?
- Can my leadership skills be improved?

Obviously, these are only some of the questions that concern today's conscientious coach. In chapter 1, we defined leadership as the process of guiding your program and supervising your athletes. In this chapter, we examine the concept of leadership as it applies to coaching, take a brief look at some popular theories of leadership, and then focus our attention exclusively on a workable approach to developing leadership skills. If you take a practical rather than a theoretical approach to leadership behavior, you will be able to utilize the following information to develop your leadership skills, which in turn will greatly enhance your coaching effectiveness.

COACHES AND LEADERS

Before proceeding, it is important to know the similarities and differences between the terms *coach* and *leader*. As a coach, you are by definition placed in the position of having to make decisions regarding your athletes. Stated another way, you have a legitimate power base from which to operate. This fact in itself, however, does not mean that you are automatically an effective leader. An effective leader is a person with the ability to influence people above and beyond what is normally expected from the position of authority itself. It's getting that "something extra" from your athletes because somehow you make them want to try harder. That is really what being a leader is all about.

It is important to remember that as a coach you can become an effective leader only by consciously developing the skills necessary to lead your athletes. Once you have done this, you will notice a definite improvement in your coaching effectiveness.

POPULAR THEORIES OF LEADERSHIP

A review of available literature reveals three traditional approaches to studying leadership. Let's take a brief look at these approaches and see what each has to offer the serious coach.

Trait Theories of Leadership

If you were to describe a leader based on the general comments presented in today's media, you might list qualities such as intelligence, decisiveness, charisma, enthusiasm, bravery, strength, self-confidence, and integrity. These are characteristics we can associate with some of our leaders today. Early researchers attempted to list such qualities when they studied leadership behavior (e.g., Fiedler & Leister, 1977; Gibb, 1969; Hendry, 1968). They tried to isolate particular personality traits that were common to successful leaders.

A summary of these studies indicates inconsistent conclusions and a number of dead ends. Apparently, the best that can be said of the trait theory approach is that intelligence, extroversion, self-assurance, and empathy tend to be related to achieving and maintaining a leadership position.

Over the years, trait theories have been largely dismissed as predictors of good leaders because of the following inherent limitations:

- They totally ignore the needs of the followers or athletes.
- They fail to clarify the relative importance of various traits.
- They ignore situational factors.

Although they could specify traits that almost all leaders possess, these same traits were often held by a substantial number of nonleaders as well.

The trait theories of leadership can be of some use. They give us an idea of those traits that athletes consider important in assessing leadership potential. Based on research using the trait approach, your athletes may see you as a more effective leader if you

- appear knowledgeable in your sport,
- have an outgoing personality,
- come across as confident in your coaching abilities, and
- attempt to understand how the athlete is feeling.

Behavioral Theories of Leadership

The inability to understand leadership with the trait approach led other researchers to look at the behaviors that specific leaders exhibited (e.g., Korman, 1966; Smith, Smoll, & Curtis, 1979; Stogdill & Coons, 1957). This approach questioned whether there is something unique in the way effective leaders behave. Using a technique known as factor analysis, a list of more than a thousand dimensions of leader behavior was eventually narrowed to two behavioral categories: initiating structure and consideration.

An example of initiating structure behavior from the coaching environment is the extent to which you define and structure roles in an attempt to attain a goal. You are engaging in initiating structure when you organize practice plans, delegate responsibility, formalize offensive or defensive strategies, or develop individual and group goals. Consideration, on the other hand, refers to your ability to handle coaching situations with a high degree of respect and regard for your athletes' ideas and feelings.

Although these two categories show some promise in identifying leader behaviors, they fall far short of enumerating the situational factors that influence success or failure. Once again using examples from the coaching environment, does the coach of a recreational basketball team behave the same as a coach in the NBA? Does a group of young athletes require the same leadership behaviors as a squad of varsity athletes? In each case, it seems highly unlikely. Missing in this comparison is consideration of the situational factors that influence success or failure. Because the behavioral approach could not clarify these and similar problems, researchers continued to search for a more appropriate leadership theory.

The best that can be said about behavioral theories of leadership is that they too give us some idea of those behaviors others see as important in assessing our leadership potential. Your athletes may see you as a more effective leader if you

- define and structure your coaching role and the roles of your athletes in the search for goal attainment; and
- are friendly and approachable, show a willingness to help your athletes with personal problems, and treat all your athletes equally.

Contingency Theories of Leadership

Over the years, it became increasingly clear to those studying leadership that predicting leadership success was far more complex than isolating a few traits or preferable behaviors. This failure to obtain consistent results led to a new focus on situational factors (e.g., Csoka & Bons, 1978; Fiedler, 1967; Kerr, Schriescheim, Murphy, & Stogdill, 1974). From a coaching perspective, contingency theories suggest that leadership can be summarized by the following equation:

$$L = l \times a \times s$$

This equation suggests that leadership (L) is a function of the leader's style (l), the athletes (a), and the situation (s). If any one of these factors changes, it affects the outcome, or results. Contingency theories of leadership have gained wider acceptance than have trait and behavioral theories. Once again, however, these contingency theories provide us with limited information on how to develop coaching leadership potential. Contingency theory does point out which types of skills must be developed, thereby providing the focus for the remainder of this chapter. Contingency theories hold that your leadership effectiveness in a coaching situation will improve if you

- make an effort to get to know your own particular style of leadership,
- recognize individual differences in your athletes, and
- consider the importance of situational factors in making coaching decisions.

LEADERSHIP STYLES

Although each coach has his or her own unique characteristics, these characteristics usually reside within one of three predominant leadership styles. Let's take a brief look at the types of leadership found in the sporting environment.

Directive Leadership

The major distinguishing feature of directive leadership is that the coach initiates the task structure of the athletes' work and guides them to achieve their task goals. This type of leadership is very task-oriented and primarily concerned with skill development as an end result. Less attention is given to the athletes' ideas and feelings. According to the behavioral theories of leadership discussed earlier, this type of leader is characterized as high in initiating structure and low in consideration. Coaches using directive leadership tend to

- define the athletes' or team's performance goals,
- assign responsibilities for individual athletic performance,

- establish a well-defined authority hierarchy,
- train athletes solely in terms of performance,
- provide all the necessary information and instructions, and
- use both rewards and punishments to control athlete behavior.

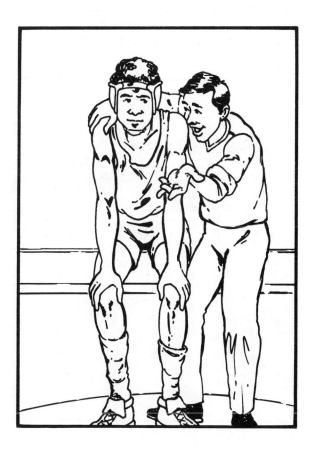

Supportive Leadership

This form of leadership is characterized by friendly, approachable, and considerate leader behavior. The coach utilizing this style is people-oriented and mainly concerned with keeping athletes happy. Less attention is devoted to structuring tasks specific to skill development. Behavioral theories of leadership characterize this type of leader as high in consideration. Coaches using supportive leadership tend to

- show personal interest in the athletes,
- be friendly and approachable,
- provide ongoing personal consultations with the athletes,
- encourage athletes to express their feelings and concerns,
- strive for harmony within the team, and
- stress positive rewards rather than punishment.

Participative Leadership

This form of leadership is often referred to as "team management" because the coach shares the responsibilities with the athletes. The coach utilizing this democratic style makes every effort to share information and power with the athletes in the decision-making process. Coaches using participative leadership tend to

- allow team members to have a voice in defining their own goals,
- permit athletes a voice in structuring their practices,
- negotiate problems or differences of opinion with athletes,
- allow team members to exercise some control over their own performance progress,
- use reward systems determined by the team as a whole (rather than only by the coach), and
- share the athletes' and team's successes and failures.

What Is Your Style?

It is important that you determine your own personal style and develop your skills in relation to it. I recommend the participative leadership style as a viable mix of task and people orientation.

A WORKABLE APPROACH TO LEADERSHIP DEVELOPMENT

Now that we have examined the various theories of leadership, their conflicting results, and three different leadership styles, it should be clear to you that the process of predicting leadership behavior does little to aid the coach in his or her day-to-day tasks. Yet, leadership techniques can be learned and developed.

In the coaching environment, leadership can be seen as consisting of three specific functions: stimulating a needed change, managing conflict, and promoting effective communication. As a coach, you can develop your leadership skills by learning and practicing a variety of techniques to use in each of these important areas. The remainder of this chapter presents a number of techniques that can help make you a more effective coach by improving your ability to interact with athletes.

Techniques to Improve Your Skill as a Change Agent

A successful coach is often responsible for stimulating change, either within the sport's governing body or within the team itself. Efforts to bring about change are frequently met with resistance, as change both threatens the investment a person has already made in the sport and increases an individual's feeling of uncertainty. Research has revealed that people dislike uncertainty; hence, most people dislike or resist change. As a serious coach, you must therefore be familiar with the best change-producing intervention techniques. Let's examine some of the more popular methods that have the potential for use in the coaching environment. You will find that these techniques work best if you have taken the time to understand your athletes.

Survey Feedback

This approach makes use of questionnaires to assess the attitudes of team members or other individuals. Use the data you collect as a springboard for future discussion and problem solving. This technique is especially valuable when information is needed to solve a particular problem. For example, you could use this procedure if you perceive an attitudinal problem among your team members. Give each athlete a questionnaire asking the following or similar questions:

- Do you feel the team has a problem that is affecting our performance?
- What specifically do you believe is the problem?
- What do you think can be done to resolve this problem?

You can then use the collected information as a starting point for discussion during a team meeting. This technique not only gathers needed information but also brings the problem out in the open so that a solution can be initiated.

As a coach you must always be looking for ways to improve your performance. Survey feedback can provide you with the information you need to become a more effective leader. A major advantage to using such feedback as a change intervention technique is that it shows your athletes you care about their opinions. It also has the advantage of providing you with valuable information that you can use to improve your coaching effectiveness. The main disadvantage of this approach is that it assumes the athletes answer your questions honestly and effectively.

Team Building

The main idea behind team building is for you to foster a high degree of interaction between team members to increase awareness, trust, and openness. This technique is of special value if the team lacks cohesion or if you perceive the need to establish new direction in your coaching efforts. Examples of team-building activities include group goal setting, the development of interpersonal relations among group members by means of more interaction, role analysis to clarify the specific responsibility to the team of each coach and athlete, and a group analysis of key processes within the team. All of these functions are performed in an effort to isolate ways to make improvements.

A common example of how to incorporate team building is the coach calling the team together to examine ways to break out of a slump. Involving all team members in open discussion enables specific problems to be identified. You can then take corrective action by designating responsibilities according to the determined needs.

A major advantage to team building is that it results in clearly defined goals for the athlete and the team. Increased motivation also results because this technique encourages group goal setting. The major disadvantage to this intervention strategy is that it is very time-consuming. The time is well spent, however, if it results in better team harmony and clearly defined performance and nonperformance goals. Both results will improve your leadership within the coaching environment.

Intergroup Development

With this particular technique, you attempt to change the attitudes, stereotypes, and perceptions that individuals or groups have toward each other. This technique can be useful, for example, if two cliques exist on your team. When using this approach, have each group meet independently to respond to three questions:

- How does your group perceive itself?
- How does your group perceive the other group?
- How do you feel the other group perceives your group?

Once you have established that the groups misunderstand each other, bring them together to unveil their misconceptions. Such a meeting can be very rewarding.

Getting both groups to go through this process can often alleviate stereotypes and false perceptions. This technique also works very well between individuals, such as the head coach and the assistant coach, or between two team members. Remember, this technique works best when *misconceptions* exist between groups or team members.

The major advantage to intergroup development is that it can quickly clear up misunderstandings that are perceptual in nature (e.g., if one group perceives they are disliked by another group when this is not really true). The disadvantage to this strategy is obvious when the perceptions are in fact valid. When this is the case, you must go back to the drawing board and try another strategy. The effective coach is always looking for ways to eliminate unproductive cliques that hinder team efficiency.

Behavior Modification

You can effect a great deal of change using behavior modification to shape, improve, and direct the behavior of team members through concentration on consequences. This strategy is valuable any time you want to develop a desirable behavior or eliminate an undesirable one.

The principle behind behavior modification is that people will most likely engage in a desired behavior if they are rewarded for doing it. These rewards are most effective if they immediately follow the desired response. Behavior that is not rewarded, or that is punished, is less likely to be repeated.

By manipulating the use of reinforcers, behavior can ultimately be changed. Examples of positive reinforcers that you could use to increase a certain behavior are verbal praise, social recognition, more playing time, and positive feedback regarding the desired behavior. Examples of negative reinforcers are punishment of any kind, verbal abuse, and negative feedback. Most authorities recommend that coaches try to stress the positive and concentrate more on positive reinforcers than on negative reinforcers. This makes the sporting environment much more enjoyable for the athlete and serves to increase athlete motivation.

The major advantage to behavior modification is that it is the most observable and measurable change technique available. It is also easy to use on an ongoing basis. The only disadvantage to behavior modification is that it requires an excellent understanding of reinforcers; otherwise it can produce results opposite of those intended. For this reason, it is important that you develop a keen understanding of behavior modification techniques. Though a complete description of behavior modification is outside the scope of this book, I encourage interested readers to consult both the *Coaches Guide to Sport Psychology* (Martens, 1987) and the *Sport Psychology Study Guide* (Bump, 1989) for additional information. This will further develop your leadership skills and overall coaching effectiveness.

Techniques to Improve Your Skill as a Conflict Manager

In any team situation, conflicts are inevitable. Handling these conflict situations properly is a major responsibility for the concerned coach. In this section, we examine five widely used approaches to conflict resolution and consider their relevance for improving our coaching leadership.

Problem Solving and Confrontation

This technique seeks resolution of disagreements through face-to-face confrontation by the conflicting parties. Problem solving is of special value when misinterpretations arise. Problems resulting from semantic misunderstandings and incorrect assumptions between team members or between an athlete and a coach can be quickly and effectively alleviated in this manner. Suppose, for example, you notice one of your athletes avoiding any type of contact with you during practice. Because this is an uncharacteristic behavior for the athlete, you would be wise to use the problem-solving technique to find out the cause of the problem.

With this method, just ask the athlete (in private) why he or she is avoiding you, or even more simply, ask him or her what's the matter. You may find that the athlete feels ashamed because he or she let you down in the last game or competition. When you assure the athlete that this is not the case, the misunderstanding will be cleared up and the problem solved. Although this is perhaps a simplified example, communication is the key to resolving misunderstandings.

A major advantage of this conflict resolution technique is that it gets the problem out in the open so that it can be addressed quickly and easily. The only disadvantage is that the problem can escalate into something worse if the coach doesn't handle the matter properly (i.e., objectively and without emotion).

Superordinate Goals

Common goals that two or more conflicting parties each desire and that cannot be reached without the cooperation of the parties involved are called *superordinate* goals. This technique is of special value in resolving conflicts between two athletes who simply don't get along. One of the more common examples of superordinate goals from the coaching environment involves team members cooperating to defeat a bitter rival. In a case such as this,

teammates who usually don't get along in practices ignore their differences long enough to join forces in an attempt to beat the opposing team. For a brief period of time, the situation itself can be seen as resolving the conflict.

As a coach, there are also times when you can initiate this procedure yourself. Try putting teammates who don't get along together well on the same side for a "two-on-two" tournament in basketball practice. Or have the conflicting parties pair up to design a specific practice session for the whole team. In this situation, the athletes have to cooperate to come up with a good practice plan, or they both look bad.

Superordinate goals are an attempt to bring conflicting athletes or coaches together by getting them to work together for a common goal. The effective leader uses this technique to reduce the amount of conflict existing within the team or sport environment. The major advantage to using the superordinate goals technique is that it fosters cooperation and teamwork rather than focusing directly on the problem itself. A disadvantage is that limited opportunities exist within the coaching environment to use this technique due to time constraints. For this reason, it is far more useful for athletic administrators than for coaches.

Avoidance

Another method of dealing with conflict is to avoid it. Although this does not offer a permanent way of resolving the conflict, it is an extremely popular short-term solution. The main value of avoidance is that it allows conflicting parties a chance to cool down. It is especially useful as an initial step until other techniques can be employed.

Avoidance is very easy to use. Conflicting individuals merely avoid contact with each other. Parents often use this technique when they tell two siblings to stay away from each other for a while, particularly when the children are fighting. In this case, the parents want the children to stay away from each other until they cool off. After some time apart, things usually return to normal.

You can also employ this technique in the coaching environment. When two athletes are really going after each other, it might be best for you to physically separate them within the practice area. In this instance, you are hoping that time will solve the problem.

Avoidance does not offer a permanent solution but can be valuable on a short-term basis when the problem is not serious or long-lasting. However, you may need to initiate another conflict resolution technique to restore the athletes' ability to work together. Keep in mind that the main advantage of avoidance is providing an immediate, short-term alternative that often prevents escalation of the problem by separating the conflicting parties. Remember, people often don't really mean the things they say in the heat of an argument. By using avoidance, the coach can prevent further development of the problem. The disadvantage of this technique, of course, is that it does not really solve the problem—it just puts it on the back burner until the issue can be resolved by another conflict-reducing strategy.

Smoothing

Smoothing can be described as the process of playing down differences that exist between individuals or groups while emphasizing common interests. This technique is also of value when individuals do not get along. This is normally accomplished in the meeting setting. The following dialogue portrays a coach utilizing the smoothing technique with two athletes.

Coach: Well, Lori and Barb, I guess you know why I asked to see you two after practice today.

Lori: C'mon, Coach. I know you mean well, but face facts. Barb and I can't stand each other, and nothing you are going to say will help.

Barb: That's the first thing she's ever said that sounds halfway intelligent.

Coach: Okay, you two, cut it out. I know you have had your differences, but you know, you both are quite a bit alike.

(Groans from both Lori and Barb.)

Coach: For example, you are two of the best athletes on my squad. You are both extremely competitive, a bit arrogant, and above all you both want what is best for the team. That's why I am confident that you two will put away your differences and help me mold this group into a championship team. After all, isn't that what we are here

for? Okay, that's all for now. Show me that my confidence in you two hasn't been misplaced.

The coach who aspires to be an effective leader must also be a bit of a politician and learn to smooth out differences that arise between the athletes. The main advantage of the smoothing technique is that it shows the athletes they have much in common. It also attempts to stress both athletes' positive features. The disadvantage of this technique is that it cannot be used if the conflicting parties have little in common.

Compromise

Compromise techniques make up a large percentage of the conflict resolution methods. The major value of compromise is that it can be used effectively when other techniques don't work. Often, external or third-party interventions result in an internal compromise between the conflicting parties. As a coach, you most likely will be called upon to be the third party, although the athletic director, team manager, or assistant coach might also assume this role.

The key to compromise is that each party must give up something of value. While there is no clear winner, there is no clear loser either. This fact in itself is likely responsible for decreasing the amount of resulting conflict.

Let's suppose that you have two athletes who just don't get along. Their constant bickering often disrupts practices. Problem solving and smoothing have done little to alleviate the situation.

In this case, you may want to consider the compromise technique. Bring the athletes together in a brief meeting after practice and ask each athlete what it is that he or she dislikes most about the other. This normally takes the form of something one person has done or said to the other person. At this point, you attempt to strike a deal. Each athlete is asked to agree that he or she will stop doing the one thing that most annoys the other. In exchange, the other athlete agrees to do the same. Although this technique doesn't solve all the problems between the conflicting parties, it often does reduce or eliminate much of the open conflict that has been disrupting your practices.

The major advantage to using compromise as a conflict management technique is that it often works when all else fails. It results in a fair solution—each party has to give up something of value. The disadvantage to this strategy is that it eliminates the symptoms of the problem but not necessarily the problem itself. A solution is reached to help the individuals live with their differences, but the main differences between the athletes still exist.

Conflict Management

When we consider the number of athletes involved in sport and the time they spend together, it becomes apparent that problems are inevitable. As a versatile coach or sport administrator, you must therefore learn to use a variety of conflict management techniques in a variety of situations. By learning to manage problem-solving confrontations and use superordinate goals, avoidance, smoothing techniques, and compromise, you can resolve individual and situational problems as they occur. This ability will greatly improve your leadership effectiveness and in the process make you a more effective coach. You can read more about this vital area in the ACEP Sport Psychology Course (Bump, 1989; Martens, 1987).

Techniques to Improve Your Skill as a Communicator

Ideas can be conveyed only when meaning is transmitted from one person to another. The coach who is a poor communicator is therefore certain to have limited effectiveness. Although perfect communication is an ideal that can never be achieved, the use of feedback and the development of good listening skills appear exceptionally beneficial in improving overall communication skills. Each technique is briefly examined here.

Feedback

The use of feedback improves the communication process and reduces the chance of major discrepancies between the information or idea received and the one intended. You can facilitate feedback by asking players to describe in their own words what they think you just said. A similar technique could be utilized by asking a team member to provide a short,

written report indicating his or her interpretation of your message. Of course, using the written alternative increases the delay between the original communication and determining whether it was received as intended. Regardless of the technique, it is important for the communicator to receive some type of feedback signaling whether the intended message was received.

Feedback has been described as one of two remedies for dealing with distorted communications. The other recommendation concerns the use of repetition. By repeating a message using various media, different formats (e.g., oral communication, written memos, monthly reports, etc.), and different words, there is a much greater chance that the idea is interpreted correctly. An example in this regard is the use of playbooks, oral presentations, and team meetings to discuss strategies.

Improving Listening Skills

Ineffective communication is most frequently thought to be the fault of the message sender. However, one of the most necessary communication skills often taken for granted is listening. Unless they have consciously worked to develop this ability, most coaches are poor listeners. With a little effort, most coaches can improve their ability as empathic listeners. This can be accomplished by observing the following guidelines:

- While listening, do not make value judgments.
- Allow the speaker to express his or her points fully before reacting.
- Do not second-guess the speaker.
- Separate objective from subjective information. Attempt to recognize the feelings and emotions in the speaker's message.
- Utilize feedback to restate the other person's position in your own words (this is usually necessary when emotions get out of hand).

When these suggestions are put into practice, the result is much more efficient communication. You will also set a good example, thereby encouraging your athletes to improve their own listening abilities. Once you have mastered these communication skills, you will be well on your way to becoming a more effective leader and coach.

MOTIVATION: A FINAL CONSIDERATION IN COACHING LEADERSHIP

One of the coach's most important responsibilities is to motivate all support staff to put forth their best efforts on behalf of the organization. This involves encouraging such individuals as assistant coaches, bus drivers, volunteers, parents, custodians, and others to do their best for the good of the team. To maintain a highly motivated staff, you must observe certain motivational principles. For example, research suggests that it is a mistake to assume that staff members are motivated solely by money. Although financial gain is certainly important, several other factors can determine an individual's degree of motivation. The most important of these are a sense of accomplishment, a feeling of belonging, recognition, and a sense of responsibility. Each person involved with your organization needs to feel that he or she is important as an individual. For this reason, the human relations skills discussed in chapter 1 take on additional significance. By taking the time to treat each staff member as an individual with individual needs, you are creating a satisfying working environment. This type of setting is most often associated with a highly motivated staff. Always remember to stress the positive and make a conscious effort to reward motivated behavior. In dealing with support staff, remember the old cliché: "You catch more flies with honey than you do with vinegar."

For a more thorough analysis of human motivation, which is beyond the scope of this book, I encourage you to consult the *Coaches Guide to Sport Psychology* (Martens, 1987) and *Motivation: Implications for Coaching and Teaching* (Carron, 1984).

SUMMARY AND RECOMMENDATIONS

Successful sport teams usually have one major ingredient that sets them apart from unsuccessful teams—dynamic and effective leadership. Over the years several theories of leadership have evolved. Although these theories have helped us understand the leadership process, they have done little to show us how to develop leadership skills. This chapter approaches leadership from an observable and workable perspective and outlines specific techniques that can be used in your efforts to become an effective leader. In considering these leadership functions, pay special attention to the following recommendations:

1. To be an effective coach, you must also be an effective leader. For this reason, it is important that you take time to develop the skills presented.
2. Trait theories of leadership suggest that your athletes will view your leadership favorably if you appear knowledgeable in your sport, are outgoing in nature, convey confidence in your coaching abilities, and attempt to understand your athletes' feelings.
3. Behavioral theories of leadership indicate that you will be seen as a more effective leader if you define and structure your coaching role and the roles of your athletes and if you are friendly and approachable. *Show* rather than tell your athletes that you care.
4. Contingency theories of leadership recommend that you make an effort to get to know your own particular style of leadership, recognize individual differences in your athletes, and always consider the situational factors when making coaching decisions.
5. As a coach you are often responsible for bringing about needed change in your team or sport organization. Use the methods presented in this chapter to enhance your coaching effectiveness.
6. Another important role you will be asked to play is that of conflict manager. A variety of conflict resolution techniques were outlined in this chapter. Practicing these methods will reduce much of the conflict that often diverts energies from your coaching goals.
7. Always remember that you must practice the techniques described to become effective. Why not start right now in attempting to master these methods? Doing so will go a long way toward improving your leadership and overall coaching effectiveness.
8. For more information on developing communication and leadership skills, consult the ACEP Sport Psychology Course (Bump, 1989; Martens, 1987).

Chapter 7
Designing Effective Controls for Your Sport Program

Control is the final link in the functional chain of coaching administration. In the control process, you check on activities to ensure that they are going as planned and, in those instances where there are significant deviations from your planned course of action, take the necessary measures to correct the problem.

THE CONTROL PROCESS

Control can be defined as the process of monitoring activities to determine whether individual athletes and the team as a whole are obtaining and utilizing their resources effectively in order to accomplish their goals. If the goals are not being achieved, you must take corrective action. In other words, if the athletes or the team is not accomplishing the goals determined in the planning process, you must then take steps to get the athletes back on track.

The control process is made up of three separate and distinct steps. Let's look at each of these individually and see how it can be used to improve your coaching performance.

Measure the Actual Performance

The first step in control is measuring. Four common sources of information coaches frequently use to measure actual performance are personal observation, statistical reports, oral reports, and written reports. Each of these has particular strengths and weaknesses; however, combining these sources increases both the amount of input and the likelihood that you will receive reliable information.

What you measure is probably more critical to the control process than how you measure; the things you measure determine to a great extent what athletes on the team attempt to concentrate on. For example, if you stress measuring defensive skills, then the athletes will attempt to concentrate on movements that influence defensive statistics. Keep in mind that you should establish the focus in the planning (goal-setting) phase.

You must try to quantify subjective criteria and determine what value a particular type of skill has to the total team effort. Then it becomes easier to break the entity into objective segments. For example, instead of using a general subjective goal such as "to improve the defense," focus on measuring specific defensive statistics. This makes the comparison process and ultimate control more objective. Following up on this example, it is better to restate the goal as "to increase the number of forced turnovers" or "to decrease our points-against average." Specific and measurable goals such as these are far easier to control. (See chapter 2 for more information on effective goal setting.)

Compare It With a Standard

The comparison process involves determining the degree of difference between actual performance and the performance that is desired. The comparison step requires that the standard be known, that actual performance be measured, and that guidelines exist for determining the extent of allowable tolerances. Using the previous example, you need only compare the defensive statistics in a particular game to the predetermined standard set in your goals to ascertain whether your team performed satisfactorily.

Correct Any Significant Deviation

The third and final step in the control process is the action that controls the deviation. It is an attempt to adjust the actual performance, the standard, or both. You can take two distinct types of corrective action. One is immediate and deals predominantly with symptoms. For example, if your offensive system is not working adequately, you could switch to a new offense. This type of action could be described as merely "putting out the fires." The other type of corrective action gets to the root of the deviation and seeks to adjust the differences permanently. Using the same situation, team conditioning, the athletes' stage of skill development, or some other cause may be responsible for the breakdown in the original offensive system. Corrective action in this case may involve adjustments in practice planning or even a redesign of the yearly training plan.

All steps in the control process assume that standards already exist. This highlights the fact that *planning must precede control*. Standards by which control occurs are developed in your planning process. Once established, however, the functions of planning and control become a two-way street. An effective control system provides valuable feedback that can be used for refining your original plans. For example, if your win/loss record is not as good as expected, or if the team's offensive output falls consistently short of your present standards, your expectations may just be too high. A certain amount of flexibility is required in the controlling function. You should not automatically make major changes in your training program just because a particular standard is not met. Remember to check your standards first to see if they are realistic. If they aren't, this factor in itself is probably responsible for the particular goal not being met. By redefining your accepted standard of performance, you and your team will be back on track toward eventual goal attainment.

BUDGETING AS A CONTROL DEVICE

At this point, we turn our attention to another type of control—the budget. Traditionally, the process of budgeting has been viewed as an administrative paper-shuffling endeavor. It entails looking at last year's revenues and expenditures and merely projecting from these figures to come up with a new set of financial restrictions. By simply considering expected additions and deletions to your sporting program and adding an inflationary "fudge factor," your task is to itemize the information and then prepare a written report outlining the income and expenditures for the new fiscal year. Looked upon in this light, the budget seems little more than a set of financial guidelines that loosely directs the sport organization's functions. Although this technique (known as line-item budgeting) was adequate in the past when monies were readily available, it is rapidly becoming obsolete in the current era of financial restrictions.

Today, the coach and sport administrator must consider new planning techniques to help avoid the ever-increasing number of program cutbacks. By necessity, the budgeting process will evolve from a control device into a viable program planning tool. The remainder of this chapter outlines a budgeting technique that has special relevance to the area of sport administration. The process of zero-base budgeting is examined in detail, with special attention given to its potential use by the coach.

Budgeting as a Planning Tool

As mentioned in the preceding section, budgeting has traditionally been viewed as simply a control device, in that budgets are designed to guide a unit's financial actions and provide feedback if the budget is exceeded. When you keep a running record of actual revenues and expenditures and compare those figures to the present budget, your organization's functions are controlled within certain financial guidelines.

In addition to being a control device, however, budgeting has even more practical significance when used as a planning tool. Used in this manner, it forces you to evaluate the total program and justify each item's existence in the formal budget. This obviously serves the function of establishing overall program goals and priorities. It also points out areas that can

be deleted from the budget because they are not contributing to your organization's overall goals.

THE ZERO-BASE BUDGET

Zero-base budgeting (Leith, 1983) is now being praised as a revolutionary approach to establishing sport program priorities and reducing inefficiencies. As the name implies, zero-base budgeting begins with no funds allocated. You must justify your budget requests in detail without any reference to the previous level of funding. In other words, as the individual in charge of budgeting, you must be able to explain why a particular amount of money should be allocated for each activity. This forces you to identify and evaluate all activities and rank them in order of importance. It also forces you to ensure that each program and service is effective in meeting team or organizational goals and is being operated efficiently. When this is not the case, the program or activity should be replaced by a higher priority item, or the current budget should be modified accordingly.

The major difference between this technique and more traditional methods is that in the zero-base system, each coach or sport administrator begins the budgeting process with absolutely no money guaranteed to the program. In other budgeting methods a fixed-dollar amount is granted, but in the zero-base budget each item of the sport program must be completely justified before any financial allocation is granted. In this manner, inefficient budget requests are not perpetuated, and the temptation to spend leftover funds from one year to keep that allocation in future years is alleviated. Program objectives and goals are also reevaluated and updated before each budget submission.

From this general description, we can note three obvious advantages of using the zero-base budgeting system. First, this technique forces you to establish program objectives, goals, and priorities. Second, it does not allow inefficiencies to be perpetuated. If a particular item does not stand up under cost-benefit analysis, it is deleted. Third, this budgeting process creates a "feedback loop" between the planning and controlling functions, as suggested in chapter 1. Stated another way, in zero-base budgeting, if a particular item in the budget does not produce the desired results, the planning process deletes the item and establishes a new priority to take its place. This new item is then subsequently evaluated in the same manner. The feedback process ensures ongoing program evaluation and viability.

The major disadvantage to the zero-base budgeting system is that its development can be relatively time-consuming in large sport organizations. However, most administrators feel that the benefits more than justify the time spent.

Steps in the Zero-Base Process

A review of related literature indicates that the zero-base budgeting system is made up of four basic steps: identifying the decision-making unit, preparing unit budget requests, evaluating and ranking the requests, and preparing the annual budget. These sequential stages are schematically represented in Figure 7.1.

Identifying the Decision-Making Units

Decision-making units are any groupings within an organization that have the authority and responsibility for planning and controlling financial resources, including division heads or coordinators of a specific set of functions, facilities, or activities. Specific examples are such diversified personnel as athletic directors, athletic facility managers, and head coaches in charge of running an organization. In a high school setting, head coaches are the decision-making units, each reporting to the department head.

Preparing Unit Budget Requests (Decision Packages)

The decision package is the building block of the zero-base concept. It is a document that identifies and describes the needs of each decision-making unit in a manner that allows those making the final decisions to evaluate them, compare them to those of competing units, and ultimately approve or deny the budget items. As an example, a hockey head coach might identify general categories within the budget such as staffing needs, equipment and facility requirements, and competition and travel costs. He or she would then list specific requirements within each category. Staffing needs might include requests for hiring a full-time assistant coach, a team manager, and an athletic trainer. Equipment and facility needs could include requests for additional hockey sticks, new team uniforms, and rental of additional ice time. Competition and travel costs could include travel to the national championships, tune-up competition, and a midseason Christmas tournament.

Once you have identified decision packages and the specific budget requests within each of these packages, you must now turn your attention to justifying each request in detail. This entails providing the following specific types of information:

- A description of what you need
- A statement of why you need these requested items
- A list of what objectives the requested items will serve
- The proposed costs and benefits of your budget requests
- Alternate means of accomplishing your objectives if the request is denied

By providing the above information for each budget item, you are giving management the means for making objective decisions concerning your sport organization's financial requests. In preparing your budget, remember that you are just one of several units submitting financial requests, so don't be surprised if some of your items are refused.

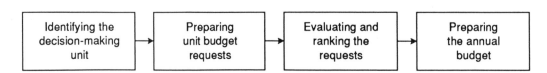

Figure 7.1. An overview of the zero-base budgeting system.

Evaluating and Ranking
the Budget Requests

Ultimately, administrative decision making involves weighing alternatives. In this step, the coach ranks his or her budget requests in each of the general categories established. Using the previous example, the hockey coach would prioritize the three items listed in each category. After this is done, a very crucial stage in the budgeting process occurs—ranking all items referred to in the budget in order of importance. Continuing with our hockey example, the coach should rank all nine requests in order of overall importance to the team or sport organization.

For the sake of clarity, this step in the budgeting process involves (a) ranking budget items within each general category and (b) ranking all budget items across the different categories. This process is schematically represented in Figure 7.2.

As can be seen in Figure 7.2, the ranking of items occurs initially within each category and finally between categories. In this example, hiring a team trainer, securing additional ice time, and travel to the national championships are seen as top-priority items within their respective categories. However, in the overall ranking process, the coach must prioritize *all* the items in terms of their potential for actualizing the organization's objectives and goals.

A brief glance at the hockey example indicates that the coach in this particular instance feels that additional practice time is paramount to the team's success. Hiring a trainer to help keep the team healthy and funding to attend the national championships are seen as second and third priorities, respectively. This process continues until each budget item is recorded in the overall ranking.

Because each budget item has been outlined along the five dimensions described in

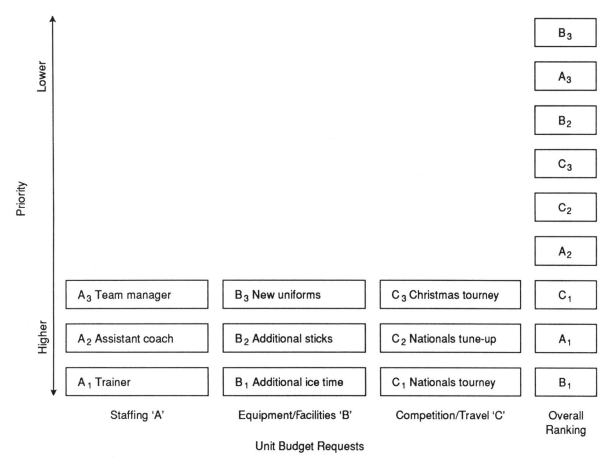

Figure 7.2. An example of the zero-base budgeting process as applied to athletics.

the preceding section, the final decision package provides the funding agent with adequate information to objectively consider each request in detail. Rather than needing to speculate the reason for each item's inclusion in the budget request, the final financial decision maker has all the necessary information at his or her fingertips.

Preparing a Detailed Operational Budget

Once you have prioritized your budget requests, the next step is to prepare a detailed budget for the selected items. This finalized submitted budget need not look any different than the one arrived at by more traditional budgeting techniques. The key difference, however, is the process, or the means by which the final submission is obtained.

PUTTING IT ALL TOGETHER

The process of control enables you to determine whether your predetermined objectives and goals are being met. This requires that you measure actual performances, compare them to standards that you established in the planning process, and take corrective action when it is needed. Control is the mechanism that tells you if your coaching efforts have been effective. For this reason, this often overlooked process is vitally important to coaching development. Indeed, it provides you with the necessary feedback to continue improving your coaching effectiveness.

Because of the ever-increasing financial constraints on today's sports, budgeting has become an important form of control. This chapter dealt exclusively with zero-base budgeting because of its value as both a planning and a control device.

As a guideline, most coaches need to include the general categories shown in Table 7.1 in their budget requests. The exact items will vary from one sport organization to another, but the general categories serve as valuable reference points.

Assuming you are the decision-making unit, feel free to use the worksheet on page 65 to identify and justify your unit budget requests. After this has been done, use the worksheet on page 66 to evaluate and rank your

Table 7.1
General Budget Categories
With Sample Items

Budget category	Sample expenditures
Salaries/wages	Assistant coach, trainer, student assistants, referees/officials, janitors, etc.
Travel	Team transportation, hotel accommodations, meals
Equipment	Baseballs, bats, basketballs, uniforms, nets, chalk, etc.
Maintenance and repair	Field maintenance, scoreboard repair, equipment repair, etc.
Facility rental	Fieldhouse, playing fields, swimming pools, ice rink, etc.
Miscellaneous	Continuing education (courses, clinics), telephone, printing, advertising, dry cleaning, team insurance, etc.

budget requests. (Refer back to Figure 7.2 as a review of this procedure.)

SUMMARY AND RECOMMENDATIONS

As you examine the control process and its relevance for making you a more effective coach, keep the following recommendations in mind:

1. Without the control process, you have no way of knowing if your coaching objectives and goals are being met. For this reason, it is very important for you to develop a thorough control process for your sport organization.
2. For the control stage to be effective, you must have objectives and goals that are observable, measurable, and realistic. You are encouraged to review the material in chapter 2 when devising your approach to control.
3. If you perform your measurement and find a particular standard is not being met, first ask yourself if the predetermined standard was realistic. This

Budget Worksheet 1
Identifying Unit Budget Requests

Budget category (decision package)	Requested items (be specific)	Purpose of requests (objective)	Proposed costs of requests	Proposed benefits of requests	Alternate means of accomplishing objectives
Salaries/ wages					
Travel					
Equipment					
Maintenance/ repair					
Facility rental					
Miscellaneous					

Budget Worksheet 2
Evaluating and Ranking Budget Requests From Worksheet 1

6.

5.

4.

3.

2.

1.

Package #1
(Salaries/wages)

6.

5.

4.

3.

2.

1.

Package #2
(Travel)

6.

5.

4.

3.

2.

1.

Package #3
(Equipment)

6.

5.

4.

3.

2.

1.

Package #4
(Maintenance/repair)

6.

5.

4.

3.

2.

1.

Package #5
(Facility rental)

6.

5.

4.

3.

2.

1.

Package #6
(Miscellaneous)

16.

15.

14.

13.

12.

11.

10.

9.

8.

7.

6.

5.

4.

3.

2.

1.

Overall ranking

can save you a great deal of time and needless energy revising your training program.

4. Because of today's financial restrictions, as a coach you will feel increasing pressure to justify your expenditures. For this reason, familiarize yourself with the latest creative budget-making techniques.

5. Consider using zero-base budgeting. It forces you to evaluate your program and eliminate those activities that are not contributing to your overall coaching objectives and goals.

Chapter 8
Making Effective Decisions

As coaches, we invariably find ourselves in the position of having to make decisions, decisions, and more decisions. We have to decide which athletes will make the team; we have to choose the starting lineup; we have to determine how many practices to have each week and how they should be structured; we have to decide which factors will lead to peak performance; and so on. It's hard to imagine a day going by when a coach doesn't have to make a decision.

DAVIS...HMM??...JAMES

WHAT IS DECISION MAKING?

Decision making is the means by which coaches plan, organize, lead, and control. A brief glance at all the examples cited reveals that the essence of decision making is *choice*. When we talk about making decisions, we mean that we have two or more alternatives from which to choose. However, the choice we ultimately make is really the product of a larger process that involves determining the need for a decision as well as developing and evaluating alternatives. Decision making, then, is a multistep process that results in selecting one alternative over another.

TYPES OF DECISIONS

You need to make different types of decisions as a coach. Sometimes you have to choose to do something different (an active decision), such as change your basic practice plan. At other times you may decide to stay with your original choice (a passive decision). You're also involved in situations where decisions are routine and repetitive (a programmed decision), as in violations of rules. Or you may face very unique circumstances (a nonprogrammed decision). Let's investigate these alternatives.

Active Versus Passive Decisions

Decision making can be an active process, like when you make a choice to do something different. For example, if one of your athletes no longer shows the improvement with training that you expect, you would probably make some changes to get the athlete back on track.

Although changing something is what normally comes to mind when we think about decision making, the definition could also include passive decisions. *Passive decision making* involves maintaining the status quo. The old cliché "not to decide is to decide" adequately sums up passive decision making. By deciding to do nothing, you are in actuality deciding to keep doing the same thing. Using the previous example, if your athlete is no longer showing adequate improvement, you may simply decide to let the situation continue in the hope that he or she will work out of the slump.

Which technique to use obviously depends on a variety of factors, such as length of the slump, the athlete's motivation, the perceived reason for the lack of improvement, the athlete's previous history, and your own personal experience with problems of this nature.

Programmed Decisions

Because programmed decisions are repetitive and routine, a definite approach has been worked out so that you do not have to treat these as new or unusual each time they occur. Given a certain known situation, you need only react with a learned and appropriate response. Some common examples of programmed decisions in the coaching environment include the following.

Objectives

These are the goals toward which your sport program is directed. Examples of objectives include reducing the number of sport dropouts; reducing the number of "goals against" by 20%; or maintaining an *Athletes First, Winning Second* philosophy. Objectives establish a common set of expectations among the athletes and can be used as guidelines in making day-to-day decisions. Be sure to review goal setting in chapter 2, and in the *Coaches Guide to Sport Psychology* (Martens, 1987).

Standards

Stated simply, standards are criteria against which something can be compared. A state meet qualifying time for the mile run is an example of a standard that can be used to decide who is allowed to participate in that particular event. Requiring varsity athletes to maintain passing grades is another example of a standard that can be used to make coaching decisions. In both cases, a standard must be met before the athlete is allowed to participate. This makes the decision for you.

Procedures

A procedure is a series of interrelated steps that must be performed in the proper order to achieve the desired results. In chapter 5 we examined procedures for setting up a variety of athletic competitions. Another common example from the coaching environment is the initial procedure for treating a sport injury (RICE—Rest, Ice, Compression, and Elevation). These steps follow a specific procedure and lead to the desired end result. Procedures for teaching sport skills described in *Coaching Young Athletes* (Martens, Christina, Harvey, & Sharkey, 1981), *Coaches Guide to Teaching Sport Skills* (Christina & Corcos, 1988), and *Successful Coaching* (Martens, 1990) are further examples of this nature. To prevent you from having to decide how to proceed each time, a common set of guidelines has been developed for your use.

Rules

Rules are explicit statements that tell the athlete what he or she can and cannot do. Classic examples include "no smoking," "no drinking," and "lights out by 11:00 P.M." Each of these examples leaves no room for judgment or individual discretion. A rule is a rule! By establishing rules such as these, you are not forced to decide on an appropriate action each time the situation comes up. It has already been decided that these behaviors are not allowed, and appropriate penalties have already been established.

Policies

Policies are general guides to decision making that allow you to utilize your judgment within certain limits. For example, if you made it a rule to require 100% attendance at practices, there could be no exceptions. As I mentioned before, a rule is a rule. Policies, however, allow you to make necessary exceptions. Sickness or a death in the family are examples of acceptable excuses for missing a practice.

Another example is provided in chapter 2 where we discussed athletic equipment purchasing policies. These policies provide you with general guidelines for buying equipment. The extent to which you follow these policies is a matter of personal choice, based on your past experience. As a coach, you must carefully consider whether a rule or a policy will best serve the interests of the team and individual athletes.

Nonprogrammed Decisions

All of the previous examples represent techniques of programmed decision making. Sometimes, though, you must make decisions concerning situations that are relatively novel and unstructured. No clear-cut solution exists for handling the problem because either it has never occurred before, or it is so complex, vague, or important that it deserves a custom-made treatment. Some examples of these nonprogrammed decisions in the coaching environment include programs, strategies, and budgets.

Programs

A program is a variety of plans for achieving your objectives. Every coach should develop a structured program to improve the performance of his or her athletes. A common example in this regard is the development of a yearly training program for the athletes. In this plan, physical, psychological, and social elements are combined to form an integrated blueprint for athlete development. Any program should contain all the activities necessary for achieving the objectives and should clarify who should do what and when it should be done. Obviously, one standard program cannot be developed because the sport, level of competition, objectives, and individual athletes vary from one situation to another. For this reason, a program can be referred to as a nonprogrammed form of decision making. It is tailor-made for each situation.

Strategies

Strategies are plans that react to or take into consideration the actions of others. A common example is the coach who leads his or her team into a basketball final against a much taller team. In this case, the coach has to develop a plan to neutralize the other team's height advantage, thereby taking away their major strength. Effective strategies in this case would be utilizing a fast-break type of offense and "pressing" the opposing team most of the

game. With this strategy, you have formulated an effective plan that can counter the other team's height advantage.

The area of sport psychology provides the coach with more examples of this type of plan. Precompetition and competition coping strategies attempt to provide the athlete with flexibility of action under a variety of situations. Utilizing this type of mental preparation puts teams as well as individual athletes in a better position to react to potentially upsetting circumstances in the sporting environment. This type of nonprogrammed decision making is becoming very popular in the pursuit of athletic excellence.

Budgets

One of the most common nonprogrammed decision-making guides is the budget. Because financial circumstances as well as program objectives vary from one sporting situation to another, the budget is unique to each particular sporting organization. When your budget is planned, you are actually making nonprogrammed decisions about the direction your team will take in the coming year. You have determined how your money will be spent to best accomplish your objectives. Because of the importance of effective budgeting, this topic was dealt with in detail in chapter 7.

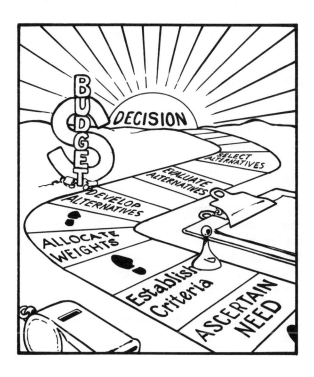

THE DECISION-MAKING PROCESS

So far, this chapter has focused on several tools that can actually reduce the number of decisions that you must spontaneously make during the course of a season. Sometimes, however, a specific decision cannot be avoided. The remainder of this chapter provides you with a decision-making technique that will eliminate much of the subjectivity that often accompanies the decision-making process.

An area from the world of business administration known as management science provides an excellent technique for making active coaching decisions. The following list outlines the six steps in the decision-making process:

1. Ascertain the need for a decision.
2. Establish decision criteria.
3. Allocate weights to the criteria.
4. Develop alternatives.
5. Evaluate the alternatives.
6. Select the best alternative.

Let's take a look at an example of how we could use this decision-making process in the world of coaching.

Step 1: Ascertain the Need for a Decision

The decision-making process begins when you determine that a problem exists or that an unsatisfactory condition is present. This is usually the case when a discrepancy exists between what is and what should be (as established in the planning process). In other words, your established objectives or goals are not being met. For example, suppose the coach of a soccer team has established the objective of improving the team's win/loss record in this year's regular season. Midway through the season, however, the team's record is slightly worse than it was last year. If the original objective was realistic, then a problem obviously exists. The coach must now make a decision regarding how to get the team's winning percentage back on schedule. In sum, then, the decision-making process begins when you recognize that a gap exists between what is desired and what is actually taking place.

Step 2: Establish Decision Criteria

Once you have determined the need for a decision, you then establish decision criteria. This merely involves identifying those factors that will be important in making your decision. Taking our previous example, the coach has determined that he must make a decision regarding how to improve his team's league performance. At this stage, the coach must now create a list of criteria that will have to be met for the team to improve its league standing. This really involves determining what factors will lead to improved performance.

Using the same example, let's say that the coach has identified six necessary criteria that must be met if the team is going to meet its preseason objective of improving its league performance. The criteria for improving the team's performance are outlined below:

- Better competition
- Improved conditioning
- Better mental preparation
- Improved technical skills
- More elaborate game strategy
- Increased athlete motivation

This list identifies those areas the coach thinks the team needs to develop further. Because of your close working relationship with your athletes, you are obviously in the best position to develop such a list.

Step 3: Allocate Weights to the Criteria

You must now prioritize the list of criteria. Because some of these factors are certainly going to be more important than others, each criterion must be assigned a "weight" (from 1 to 10) to reflect its perceived importance in helping meet the objective. When weighting the criteria, keep in mind that larger numbers indicate greater importance and smaller numbers reflect lesser importance. Let's say the coach chooses the weights shown in Table 8.1. Table 8.1 indicates that in this particular situation, the coach feels that better competition (in the form of exhibition games) is the most important criterion for improving the team's win/loss record within the league. Athlete motivation also appears to be a high

Table 8.1
Coach's Weighting of Criteria
for Improving Team Performance

Criteria	Weight (1-10)
Better competition	9
Improved conditioning	6
Better mental preparation	4
Improved technical skills	7
More elaborate game strategy	2
Increased athlete motivation	8

priority. A more elaborate game strategy is perceived as the least important factor in the established list of criteria.

It is important to note that different coaches might perceive different criteria as more important than the ones listed in this example. They might also weight the same criteria differently. This points out the individual nature of decision making. The criteria and the weights selected merely reflect the factors that individual coaches perceive to be important in the particular decision at hand. The weightings are a product of the coach's experience, knowledge, and available resources and the unique situation at hand.

Step 4: Develop Alternatives

At this point, the coach must proceed to develop a list of alternatives that can fulfill the criteria established in Step 2. This particular phase of the decision-making process draws on the coach's knowledge and experience in identifying viable alternatives. Following up on our example, let's suppose four potential alternatives have been formulated to lead to improvement in the areas previously mentioned:

- More tournament play
- Increased practice time
- Utilize a sport psychologist
- Return to basics (technical skills)

In the next step these alternatives are evaluated.

Step 5: Evaluate the Alternatives

Once the alternatives have been established, each must be critically evaluated. In our example, this step involves ranking (from 4 to 1) the four alternatives in terms of their ability to fulfill each of the six criteria. A ranking of 4 indicates that this alternative is considered the best way to improve the criterion; a ranking of 1 indicates the least effective alternative. In our example, the coach has ranked each alternative as illustrated in Table 8.2.

According to the table, the coach determines that more tournament play (4), increased practice time (3), a return to basics (2), and the use of a sport psychologist (1) will (in that order) result in better competition. This same ranking process is then performed on each individual criterion as summarized in Table 8.2.

Table 8.2
Coach's Ranking of Alternatives Against Each Criterion

Criteria/alternatives	More tournament play	Increased practice time	Utilize a sport psychologist	Return to basics
Better competition	4	3	1	2
Improved conditioning	2	4	1	3
Better mental preparation	3	2	4	1
Improved technical skills	2	3	1	4
More elaborate game strategy	4	2	1	3
Increased athlete motivation	3	2	4	1

Step 6: Select the Best Alternative

The final step in the decision-making process involves multiplying each alternative's ranking by the corresponding criterion weighting. This step is summarized in Table 8.3. For example, in the first row, the numbers 36, 27, 9, and 18 are determined by multiplying the criterion weighting shown at the left of the table by the individual rankings of the alternatives shown in Figure 8.2. Now add up the numbers under each alternative to get a total sum. The alternative with the highest number is the correct decision. In this case, the decision-making process has determined that playing more tournaments will best result in improved overall performance. Because increased practice time is a close second, the coach may want to use this alternative as well.

To this point we have assumed that the coach can add more tournaments to the schedule. Now the coach must be creative to juggle this decision with the budget and league regulations.

The decision-making process is an objective way of making active coaching decisions. Rather than forcing coaches to rely on subjective feelings, this process provides an administrative tool for determining the best course of action. Although we looked at only one example, you can use this process any time an extremely important decision is required. Other times, you will be able to rely on the various forms of programmed decisions outlined earlier in this chapter.

SUMMARY AND RECOMMENDATIONS

This chapter made several recommendations regarding effective decision making in the coaching environment. Remember, decision making is the tool you utilize to plan, organize, lead, and control, so review the following recommendations carefully:

1. Being an effective coach involves making a large number of important decisions. For this reason, you must be aware of the successful decision-making techniques.
2. Be sure to carefully develop objectives, standards, procedures, rules, and policies. This avoids having to treat related decisions individually later in the season. The time and effort you save can be focused on more important concerns, such as skill development and improved player relations.
3. Use the six-step decision-making process as a tool for making objective decisions:

   • Ascertain the need for a decision.
   • Establish decision criteria.
   • Allocate weights to the criteria.
   • Develop alternatives.
   • Evaluate the alternatives.
   • Select the best alternative.

By employing this method, the coach has a scientific technique for making effective choices. This technique is of

Table 8.3
Making the Final Decision

(Wt)	Criteria/alternatives	More tournament play	Increased practice time	Utilize a sport psychologist	Return to basics
(9)	Better competition	36	27	9	18
(6)	Improved conditioning	12	24	6	18
(4)	Better mental preparation	12	8	16	4
(7)	Improved technical skills	14	21	7	28
(2)	More elaborate game strategy	8	4	2	6
(8)	Increased athlete motivation	24	16	32	8
	Totals	106	100	72	82

special value when a very important decision is required.

4. Because effective decision making involves establishing important criteria and developing alternatives, continue to expand your knowledge and keep up with new information that can help you in the decision-making process.

Conclusion

Today's coach is under more pressure than ever before. Faced with the ever-increasing sophistication of modern-day sports, coaches must learn new ways to focus their efforts. Just as athletes continue to get better each year, coaches have to learn to do the same. Rather than sit back and react to situations as they occur, you must aggressively plan and organize your efforts to ensure an improved coaching performance. The *Coaches Guide to Sport Administration* has provided the necessary tools to approach coaching in this fashion.

At this stage, I feel it is important to note that these administrative skills are of equal value in youth, high school, and elite sport programs. Though any little edge can often make the difference between winning and losing in high-level sports, it can also make the difference between enjoying participation and dropping out at any skill level. The ACEP motto— *Athletes First, Winning Second*—places the responsibility for providing a quality coaching performance squarely on your shoulders. This applies regardless of whether you are taking an international-caliber athlete to the limits or merely making sport more fun for children. Both are equally important. For this reason, it is important to use every tool at your disposal to ensure continued high-quality participation. By developing your skills in the planning, organizing, leading, and controlling functions of coaching, your increased effectiveness will make sport more enjoyable and rewarding for your athletes.

Take up the challenge and use this *Guide* and the other *Guides* in the Master Series to improve your coaching effectiveness. Now that you have finished reading this *Guide*, work through the questions and exercises in the *Sport Administration Study Guide* (Leith, 1990). Taken together, the recommendations will go a long way toward improving your coaching effectiveness.

References

Botterill, C. (1979). Goal setting with athletes. *Sports Science Periodical on Research and Technology in Sport*, Bu-1:1-8.

Bump, L.A. (1989). *Sport psychology study guide*. Champaign, IL: Human Kinetics.

Byl, J. (1990). *Organizing successful tournaments*. Champaign, IL: Leisure Press.

Carroll, L. (1920). *Alice's adventures in wonderland*. London: Macmillan.

Carron, A. (1984). *Motivation: Implications for coaching and teaching*. London: Sport Dynamics.

Christina, R., & Corcos, D. (1988). *Coaches guide to teaching sport skills*. Champaign, IL: Human Kinetics.

Csoka, L.S., & Bons, P.M. (1978). Manipulating the situation to fit the leader's style: Two validation studies of leader match. *Journal of Applied Psychology*, **63**, 295-300.

Fiedler, F.E. (1967). *A theory of leadership effectiveness*. New York: McGraw-Hill.

Fiedler, F.E., & Leister, A.F. (1977). Leader intelligence and task performance: A test of a multiple screen model. *Organizational Behavior and Human Performance*, **20**, 1-14.

Gibb, C.A. (1969). Leadership. In G. Lindzey & E. Aronson (Eds.), *The handbook of social psychology* (pp. 216-228). Reading, MA: Addison-Wesley.

Hendry, L.B. (1968). Assessment of personality traits in the coach-athlete relationship. *Research Quarterly*, **39**, 543-551.

Jensen, C. (1983). *Administrative management of physical education and athletic programs*. Philadelphia: Lea & Febiger.

Kerr, S., Schriescheim, C.A., Murphy, C.J., & Stogdill, R.M. (1974). Toward a contingency theory of leadership based upon the consideration and initiating structure literature. *Organizational Behavior and Human Performance*, **12**, 62-82.

Korman, A.K. (1966). Consideration, initiating structure, and organizational criteria: A review. *Personnel Psychology*, **19**, 349-361.

Kozoll, C. (1985). *Coaches guide to time management*. Champaign, IL: Human Kinetics.

Leith, L.M. (1983). Zero-base budgeting—the time is right in athletics. *Sports Science Periodical on Research and Technology in Sport*, P-1:1-4.

Leith, L.M. (1990). *Sport administration study guide*. Champaign, IL: Leisure Press.

Martens, R. (1987). *Coaches guide to sport psychology*. Champaign, IL: Human Kinetics.

Martens, R. (1990). *Successful coaching*. Champaign, IL: Leisure Press.

Martens, R., Christina, R., Harvey, J., & Sharkey, B. (1981). *Coaching young athletes*. Champaign, IL: Human Kinetics.

Smith, R.E., Smoll, F.L., & Curtis, B. (1979). Coach effectiveness training: A cognitive-behavioral approach to enhancing relationship skills in youth sport coaches. *Journal of Sport Psychology*, **1**, 53-58.

Stogdill, R.M., & Coons, A.E. (1957). *Leader behavior: Its description and measurement*. Columbus, OH: Ohio State University.

Voltmer, E., Esslinger, A., McCue, B., & Tillman, K. (1979). *The organization and administration of physical education*. Englewood Cliffs, NJ: Prentice-Hall.

Supplemental Reading List

Coaching Administration

Foster, B. (1978, Summer). Business management principles applied to coaching. *Basketball Bulletin*, pp. 9-10.

Jones, G., & Bretthaurer, L. (1978). Do coaches make better administrators? *Journal of Physical Education and Recreation*, **49**(5), 32.

Katz, R. (1955). Skills of an effective administrator. *Harvard Business Review*, **33**, 33-42.

Sage, G. (1973). Coach as management: Organizational leadership in American sport. *Quest*, **19**, 35-40.

Planning

Locke, E., Saari, C., Shaw, K., & Latham, G. (1981). Goal setting and task performance: 1969-1980. *Psychological Bulletin*, **90**, 125-152.

McClements, J., & Botterill, C. (1979). Goal setting in shaping of future performances of athletes. In P. Klavora & J.V. Daniel (Eds.), *Coach, athlete, and the sport psychologist* (pp. 199-210). Toronto: University of Toronto.

McClements, J., & Botterill, C. (1980). Goal setting and performance. In R. Suinn (Ed.), *Psychology in sports: Methods and applications* (pp. 269-279). Minneapolis: Burgess.

O'Block, F., & Evans, F. (1984). Goal setting as a motivational technique. In J.M. Silva & R.S. Weinberg (Eds.), *Psychological foundations of sport* (pp. 188-196). Champaign, IL: Human Kinetics.

Organizing

Caplow, T. (1976). *How to run any organization*. New York: Holt, Rinehart, and Winston.

Mintzberg, H. (1979). *The structuring of organizations*. Englewood Cliffs, NJ: Prentice-Hall.

Robbins, S. (1980). *The administrative process*. New York: Prentice-Hall.

Organizing Fund-Raisers

Ardman, H., & Ardman, P. (1980). *Woman's Day book of fund raising*. New York: St. Martins.

Brakely, G. (1980). *Tested ways to successful fund raising*. New York: ANACOM.

Bronzan, R. (1974). *New concepts in planning and funding athletics, physical education, and recreation facilities*. St. Paul: Phoenix Intermedia.

Bronzan, R. (1977). *Public relations, promotions, and fund raising for athletic and physical education programs*. New York: Wiley.

Drotning, P. (1979). *Putting the fun in fund raising*. Chicago: Contemporary.

Leith, L. (1984). Direct and indirect fund raising. *Sport Science Periodical on Research and Technology in Sport*, P-1:1-7.

Lohmann, R. (1980). *Breaking even*. Philadelphia: Temple University.

Organizing Competition

Bucher, C. (1979). *Administration of physical education and athletic programs.* Toronto: C.V. Mosby.

Leading

Chelladurai, P. (1981). The coach as motivator and chameleon of leadership styles. *Sports Science Periodical on Research and Technology in Sport*, Bu-2:1-7.

Challadurai, P., & Arnott, M. (1985). Decision styles in coaching: Preferences of basketball players. *Research Quarterly for Exercise and Sports*, **56**, 15-24.

Chelladurai, P., & Carron, A. (1981). Applicability to youth sports of the Leadership Scale for Sports. *Perceptual and Motor Skills*, **53**, 361-362.

Chelladurai, P., & Saleh, S. (1980). Dimensions of leader behaviour in sports: Development of a leadership scale. *Journal of Sport Psychology*, **2**, 34-45.

Dunnette, M., Campbell, J., & Hakel, M. (1967). Factors contributing to job satisfaction and job dissatisfaction in six occupational groups. *Organizational Behaviour and Human Performance*, **2**, 143-174.

Herzberg, F. (1968, January-February). One more time: How do you motivate people? *Harvard Business Review*, pp. 53-62.

Robbins, S. (1980). *The administrative process.* Englewood Cliffs, NJ: Prentice-Hall.

Controlling/Budgeting

Edginton, C., & Williams, J. (1978). *Productive management of leisure service organizations.* New York: Wiley.

Phyll, A. (1973). *Zero-base budgeting.* New York: Wiley.

Robbins, S. (1980). *The administrative process.* Englewood Cliffs, NJ: Prentice-Hall.

Decision Making

Heilbroner, R. (1976). How to make an intelligent decision. In J. Ritchie & P. Thompson (Eds.), *Organization and people: Readings, cases, and exercises in organizational behavior* (pp. 121-136). New York: West.

Robbins, S. (1980). *The administrative process.* Englewood Cliffs, NJ: Prentice-Hall.

Zeigler, E., & Bowie, G. (1983). *Management competency development in sport and physical education.* Philadelphia: Lea & Febiger.

Index

About the Author

Larry Leith is an associate professor in the Department of Physical and Health Education at the University of Toronto. He holds a cross-appointment with the Department of Behavioral Sciences, Faculty of Medicine, and has published over 60 articles on sport administration, sport psychology, and human behavior. Years of practical experience complement his theoretical training. Larry designed and implemented the sport administration stream at Lakehead University, was a college sport administrator for seven years, and coached five varsity sports at the college level.